BRICKS, STONES & STRAW

WORKING HORSES IN LIVERPOOL

PETER SLEEMAN

AMBERLEY

Waiting – statue of a Liverpool carthorse. Located outside the Liverpool Museum of Life, unveiled in May 2010. (Courtesy of Liverpool of Museum Life)

Dedicated to the memory of my son-in-law, Paul Philip Parsons, who sadly passed before the final draft of this volume was completed.

1965–2021

First published 2023

Amberley Publishing
The Hill, Stroud,
Gloucestershire, GL5 4EP

www.amberley-books.com

ISBN: 978 1 3981 1166 0 (print)
ISBN: 978 1 3981 1167 7 (ebook)

British Library Cataloguing in Publication Data.
A catalogue record for this book is available from the British Library.

Typeset in 10pt on 13pt Celeste.
Typesetting by SJmagic DESIGN SERVICES, India.
Printed in the UK.

Contents

Acknowledgements

I am fortunate enough to own a number of original documents that I was able to use in writing this book. I have also had help from a wide variety of sources. My thanks are due to Liverpool Central Library (especially the volunteer help desk staff); staff at the Museum of Liverpool, particularly Sharon Brown, curator of the land transport section; and staff at the Lancashire Archive, Preston.

Valerie Hemingway spent many hours researching the family trees and checking the accuracy of many of the facts quoted, and our friend the late Dawn Bickers researched and obtained a number of birth, marriage and death certificates. I am grateful for the considerable IT input from my son, Jonathan Sleeman, my late son-in-law Paul Parsons, and grandsons Noah Sleeman and Thomas Parsons. Thanks also go to staff at the University of Liverpool's Leahurst Campus and RCVS London.

I have made every effort to ensure that I have secured all copyright holders' permission to use material that I do not own personally. Unfortunately, some have proved impossible to locate and some parties have failed to respond at the time of writing. In cases where copyright holders feel they wish to have their material acknowledged, or I have failed to contact, I will be happy to correct any omissions at the earliest opportunity.

Research has included references to numerous publications and many books, and the collection of illustrations are from a variety of sources, including many from my own private collection.

Victoria Farm Freshfield, Sarah Makin's home until 1941.

Introduction

The motivation for writing this book originated when I inherited a Georgian corner cupboard from my mother. Inside the small drawer in the base of the cupboard was a collection of documents, all from the nineteenth century, providing a wealth of information on the work and life of a Liverpool carter named John Makin, who lived and worked in the hamlet of Grey Horse, in the Knotty Ash area, which was a rural area outside the city of Liverpool. I discovered that I am related to John Makin on my mother's side. My great-grandfather, Thomas Rimmer, married John's granddaughter, Sarah Makin, consequently making John my great-great-great-grandfather.

John was born in Huyton-with-Roby on 13 November 1803. This was shortly after the beginning of the French Revolution (1789). At the time of John's birth the Peninsular War was being fought in Europe, followed by the defeat of Napoleon and his troops by

Sarah Makin, John Makin's granddaughter.

Wellington at the Battle of Waterloo in 1815, which is in modern-day Belgium, when John was twelve years old. Earlier, in the same conflict (1805), Nelson won the famous Battle of Trafalgar, defeating the French fleet, but losing his own life during the fray. John would have been just two years old at the time so would not have remembered the event.

He would, almost certainly, have recalled the Rainhill Trials. Held in 1829 just outside Liverpool, very close to his home, they were a competition to decide which steam locomotive to choose to haul the new (1830) Liverpool to Manchester Railway. The event was won, rather easily, by George Stephenson's *Rocket*.

Similarly, he would have been aware of the Crimean War of 1853–56, although he would have been too old to serve in the army at that time. The war is probably best remembered for two major events: the Charge of the Light Brigade, at the Battle of Balaclava on 25 November 1854, resulting in troop causalities of 278 and the loss of 335 horses due to the incompetent and conflicting orders given by their commanders, and the nurse Florence Nightingale attending to injured troops at the front, forever known as 'the Lady of the Lamp'.

The whole period was characterised by the rapid and increasing industrialisation of England, commonly referred to as the 'Industrial Revolution'. This term usually refers to the period from 1760 to 1850, although the technical advances were continuous throughout the nineteenth century and beyond.

John would have been well aware of the changing economic conditions of his time as they directly affected his work and income as a carter, working close to a major industrial and commercial city.

Florence Nightingale.

John died on 12 October 1886 and was buried in his local church – St Mary's Church, Walton on the Hill. His lifetime therefore spanned the majority of the nineteenth century, a most exciting period in British history. During his lifetime no less than four monarchs occupied the English throne: George III (1760–1820), George IV (1820–30), William IV (1830–37) and Victoria (1837–1901).

This book is about the history of working horses from the earliest times. It covers working horses over the years, including working packhorses and Shire horses carrying freight in the nineteenth century. The early records of horse and man and its domestication, as well as the many areas of work where horse and man collaborated together, are also discussed.

The book explores social and economic conditions in Great Britain in the nineteenth century, along with the life and work of Liverpool carters throughout the nineteenth century. Included is the history of West Derby and the story of John Makin, his family, his life and his work with his own horse throughout his lifetime.

The final two chapters illustrate the decline in the use of heavy horses on economic grounds and describe the many areas where they can still be seen today, including work, recreation, ceremonies and therapy, adding colour, value and interest to our everyday life.

Plaque dedicated to Liverpool carters and their horses on the Throstles Nest pub, Scotland Road.

1

A History of the Working Horse

The horse, *Equus ferus caballus*, and the domesticated *Equus caballus*, which we would recognise today, evolved from the *Echippus* also defined as *Hyracotherium*, a multi-toed animal from over 50 million years ago, evolving eventually to the single-toed animal of today.

Domestication of the horse began around 3500 BC, when the horse was also hunted as a wild animal. Evidence exists from modern-day Kazakhstan from that period that shows the horse was kept for milk and meat rather than for riding – ancient postholes suggest a form of corral. Further evidence exists of domesticated horses from around 3000 BC being used for transport, possibly in the pursuit of war.

Later, around 2300 BC, the horse was being used in warfare, and by *c.* 2000 BC horses were being used for entertainment, pulling chariots in the arena and elsewhere. Evidence of horses being buried with their chariot (two-wheeled) has been found in Eastern Europe, and war chariots (two- and four-wheeled) were common by 1600 BC.

Petroglyph of a four-wheeled chariot. (Capo di Ponte, copyright Luca Giarelli)

By 1400 BC there is evidence of the use of bits for horses in charioteering, suggesting well-developed racing to entertain enthusiastic audiences, and improved control of chariots in wartime.

Around 1000 BC horse riding became common and the cavalry horse was first utilised. Saddles were introduced in AD 400 and stirrups in AD 500. The horse was first recorded in industry in AD 1000. Horses were highly valued for their strength and stamina.

William I brought over 2,000–3,000 horses when he invaded Britain in 1066. Later, King John imported sixty stallions to improve the quality of his stock. By 1530 modern flat racing had been introduced and various buildings and observation posts specifically designed for racegoers were becoming more widespread.

In 1678, the inception of the modern thoroughbred is recorded. By 1750 the horse had become increasingly used in agriculture, and around the same time national hunt racing commenced. Also on the sporting front, in 1900 equestrian sport was introduced for the first time in the Olympic Games.

However, by 1965 the role of the horse, solely in agriculture, was declining in the UK. Its peak was in 1905 with over 1.1 million animals. This is when we begin to see increased use of the horse as a recreational animal, a role the animal continues to occupy today.

Leasowe Castle by Harold Hopps, 1896. The castle was built by the Earl of Derby in 1593 to watch horse racing at Wallasey. (Courtesy of Williamson Art Gallery and Museum; Wirral Museums Service)

Leasowe Castle, now a hotel and events centre.

The records of horse numbers within the UK are notoriously unreliable. It is estimated that in 1800 there were approximately 3 million horses, and in 1850 there were over 2.5 million. Then from 1910 onwards there is a constant decline of working horses, partly due to many being requisitioned and lost in the First World War, as illustrated graphically in the film *Warhorse*, falling to 1.3 million in 1934 and 517,000 in 2017 (this includes all breeds).

For thousands of years the horse was seen to be a fundamental part of man's development, both commercially and personally. Man's willingness to provide the animal with food and water as well as shelter from the weather has been essential to reaping the benefits from domesticated horses over the years. Later the service of professionals, such as farriers and veterinary surgeons, became essential to maintaining the horse's good health and ability to work efficiently.

As a domesticated animal, the horse became an indispensable part of man's efforts to cultivate land, work in industry and as a form of personal transport, and remained so for centuries. Horses were also trained as fighting animals and have been used in warfare from days of old right up to the Second World War. And they have provided man with its fastest from of transport from ancient times to the early nineteenth century.

Horses have been an essential aid to our working life over hundreds of years. Examples include road freight, both locally and long distance, by packhorse, and horse-drawn wagons. In agriculture they were used to haul farm machinery, particularly ploughs, frequently as a working pair, releasing the ploughman from backbreaking work. They also hauled many types of machine, including fire engines. Their role as racehorses and the development of the thoroughbred system is well documented.

Improvements in the road system and the development of river and canal transport made significant inroads into packhorse customers. Another blow to the packhorse as a major source of both short- and long-distance freight carrying was the advent of the railway age, providing fast, reliable transport for both people and freight. This will be covered in greater detail in Chapter 11.

In addition to their working role, horses also provided man with milk, hide, meat, glue and pharmaceuticals from the urine of pregnant mares.

Horses have been traditionally divided into three major groups:

Hot bloods – Their special features are speed and endurance. They are typically used for racing.

Cold bloods – These include draft and Shire horses, as well as some ponies. This group were the mainstay of working horses. The draft and Shire horse was typically 16–18 hands high and weighed 700–1,000 kg. The largest horse ever recorded in this category was Sampson, documented in 1846 at 21.25 hands high, 86.5 inches high at his withers and weighing a massive 1,524 kg (*c.* 3,360 lbs). The main heavy horse breeds used in the UK are Shire, Clydesdale, Suffolk Punch and the Percheron.

Warm bloods – These breeds are particularly suitable for riding, especially for pleasure.

Pair of Percherons.

Shire horse.

Suffolk Punches.

Clydesdale horses.
(Courtesy of Jude,
CC BY-SA 2.0)

2

The Working Horse's Relationship with Man and Its Work

Agriculture

Throughout the nineteenth century there was a minimum of 1 million horses employed in agricultural activities. The numbers steadily rose during the century,

Horse-drawn reaper/binder. (Courtesy of Illinois Amish Heritage Centre)

reaching a peak of around 1.1 million in 1905. In addition to pulling ploughs, horses hauled a wide range of farm equipment, including binders, mowers, reapers and thrashers, harvesters, self rakers, muck spreaders, seed drills and, towards the end of the nineteenth century, steam-powered machines such as the steam harvester. They also hauled wagons for transporting the full range of crops grown from the fields to barns or storage units.

Forestry and Logging

Alongside agriculture is forestry and logging. Heavy horses traditionally hauled felled trees from within the forest to an area where they could be sawn or transferred to wagons or water transport. They are particularly suited to this task as they can work in confined spaces that machinery would be too big to operate in.

Horse working at logging.

Wartime

The horse has played a major role in warfare throughout the ages, from the nomadic tribes of Central Asia to the Muslim warriors of Eastern Europe, and across Europe from the seventh century and beyond.

The type of horse employed in war zones depended on their use: whether they were to be ridden or driven, used for reconnaissance, cavalry charges, raiding, communication or supply. Horses, mules and donkeys supported the front line and also took vital supplies to armies in the field.

Knights relied on them in their crusades to the Holy Land. In medieval times knights rode a specific horse known as a destrier, and the armour worn by the horse was described as barding. Knights selected their own horse to ride, primarily seeking strength, speed and stamina.

Horse cavalry at the Battle of Waterloo, 1815. (Lady Butler)

In the eighteenth and nineteenth centuries battle cavalry was in constant use, both in Europe and America. Mounted cavalry played a decisive role in defeating Napoleon at the Battle of Waterloo in 1815.

Native Americans put horses to excellent use when fighting to preserve their homelands and combating the US armies in their relentless drive westward. Highly mobile horse regiments were also crucial to both sides during the American Civil War.

A number of horses were requisitioned by the army early in the First World War. In 1914 alone 120,000 were taken, and by 1918 a total of 460,000 UK and Irish horses were so requisitioned, along with a further 600,000 imported from North America. This had a detrimental effect on the British economy, which was very dependent on horses in agriculture.

The horses were used for transport and carrying freight, supplies, food stores and ammunition. The larger animals were put to work hauling heavy guns to the front, a particularly difficult task in the appalling conditions of mud, bomb craters and the general quagmire of the battlefield. Large numbers were lost as a result of enemy fire and bombs; many died simply due to exhaustion, and some even drowned with their handlers in flooded shell holes. It has been estimated that as many as 8 million horses/mules and ponies from all combatants were killed in the conflict. In 2004, a memorial to all animals lost in conflict was placed in Hyde Park.

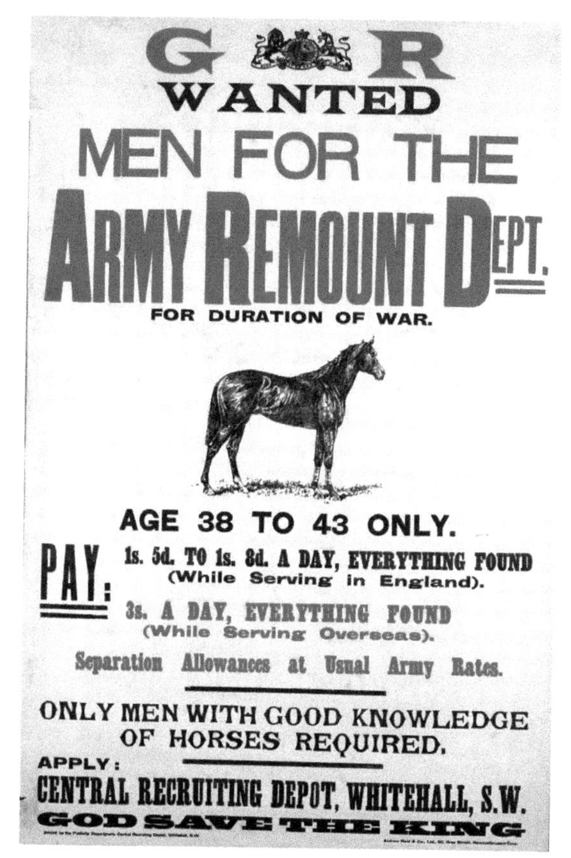

First World War recruitment poster. (Courtesy of IWM London)

Right: Blacksmith, Old Swan.

Below: Grave of Warrior, a famous First World War horse.

The Animals in War memorial, Hyde Park, London.

In spite of the major use of tanks by all sides in the Second World War, some horse cavalry units were still in use, primarily as scouts and for the transport of troops and supplies.

The US Army Special Forces even used horses in battle from 2010 in the conflict in Afghanistan. Today the use of horses in wartime is largely confined to developing countries. Elsewhere, their military use is now primarily for ceremonial and educational purposes.

Mining

Equally important economically, the working horse played a vital role in a range of mining duties. Horses, ponies and mules were employed extensively in mines in many countries. Various breeds were employed dependant on the headroom available underground. The smallest galleries used Shetlands, but Cleveland Cob, Welsh and Russian breeds and mules were also found in mines. Coal mines were the principal users from 1750 right up to 1999, but they also worked in tin and china clay mines in Cornwall.

Pit ponies' eyes shielded from working underground.

Canals

Canals employed heavy horses to pull barges for many years. A horse could pull fifty times its own weight and walk all day at a steady walking pace. The canal system was well developed by the end of the eighteenth century.

Canal working horse.

Thousands of horses were employed on canals throughout the UK. A minimum crew of two was required: one man either leading or on the horse, the other steering the boat. A heavy horse was ideal, but sometimes smaller horses were used, or a pair of donkeys. At the end of each day the horse had to be stabled and could not be left out in the cold after a hard day's work. They also had to be fed, with a high-protein feed, and watered. Some barge owners ran 'flying services', with constant changes of horse to keep the barge moving at maximum speed. Horse power was in constant use on the canal system up to the 1960s, and they are still seen on canals today for pleasure purposes.

The horse-drawn water carrier was also a frequent sight when the quality of local water was suspect. *The Liverpool Guide* of 1796 refers to water carts as the alternative supply of water from local wells, which was unacceptable even for cooking.

Horse-drawn water cart, St Austell, Cornwall. (Courtesy of Royal Cornwall Museum, Arthur Jordon)

Firefighting

Within towns and cities horses were invaluable hauling fire engines. The earliest known firefighting force was formed in 115 BC by Marcus Licinius Crassus, who made a fortune from his 500-strong firefighters in Rome. They would arrive at every known fire and do nothing until the hapless owner agreed a fee for their service.

Fire was a major hazard as many buildings were largely constructed of wood. Consequently, things were not a great deal better in seventeenth-century England, where various insurance companies provided a service to their members who had paid a fee for fire insurance and had a 'fire mark' affixed to their property as proof of payment. Other parties could engage the service by agreeing a fee, similar to the practice in ancient Rome. The horse-drawn fire engines were the quickest method of arrival, but the service was very much hit and miss, dependant on the location of the fire and the base for the horses and engines.

It was not until 1865 that the London Fire Brigade was formed and used as a model for other towns and cities, but the horse remained the unit of power throughout the nineteenth century. The horse-drawn vehicle was prevalent across a wide range of activities and was a daily sight in our towns, villages and cities, providing a service to the general public.

Horse-drawn fire engine, Birmingham, 1900. (Courtesy of *Birmingham Mail*)

Above: Horse-drawn cart, Ilkley.

Below: An unusual use of a horse – offering cleaning services. (historyofprofessionalcarpet cleaning.wordpress.com)

Brewing

Returning to commercial cargo carrying, brewers' drays were a familiar sight for hundreds of years and well into the twentieth century – usually hitched to a two-horse team. They were ideal for short journeys, as most breweries served a very limited local market. At the end of the eighteenth century Liverpool alone had thirty-eight breweries, although many would have been single pubs brewing and selling their own beer. The Joseph Jones Knotty Ash brewery operated in West Derby.

Joseph Jones Brewery advertisement. (Courtesy of David Harrison)

Brewer's dray on show demonstration.

Food Industry

An interesting use of the fast horse in the food industry occurred in France. The fishermen of Boulogne-sur-Mere, in the absence of refrigeration, needed to get their catch rapidly to the lucrative Paris markets while the fish was still fresh. They relied entirely on horses and wagons to speedily move the fish, something that became known as the 'Fish Race' or, more romantically, '*Chasse Maree*'. The concept was so popular that the race is today re-enacted every two years, to popular acclaim.

Horses also proved their worth in the dairy industry, especially in towns and cities, hauling either four-wheeled carts or two-wheeled milk floats, once again serving a limited local market within a relatively short distance from the dairy or, in many cases, farm. Cows were kept in many towns to provide fresh milk, cream, butter and cheese for their customers.

Pair of Clydesdales with a removal van in 2013 at Beamish Museum. (Courtesy of BAR)

Policing

Local authorities once used horses for crowd control in the absence of an organised police force, and frequently used mounted units of the army to put down strikes and gatherings defined illegal by the authorities. The only police service existing then were the Bow Street Runners, which were formed in 1749 but only operated in London. They also had their own horse patrol (from 1760), with members wearing bright red waistcoats as a means of identification.

After the Battle of Waterloo in 1815, times were very hard for the average family, who struggled to eke out an existence. The Corn Laws enacted in 1815 significantly increased the cost of corn and therefore bread, forcing many into poverty. In 1815, Members of Parliament comprised the wealthy and people with influence; the working man had no representation at all. Indeed, the whole system of election to Parliament was rotten to the core. A crowd of protestors 60,000–80,000 strong gathered in St Peter's Field, Manchester, on 16 August 1819 to protest their lack of representation. Although peaceful, the authorities called in the cavalry to disperse the crowd. In a massive overreaction the cavalry decided they would do this by charging the protestors, resulting in the death of fifteen and injury to another 700.

London policemen, 1829.

The event shocked the country, and Sir Robert Peel, who was later appointed Home Secretary in 1822, moved to create a proper police force in Britain in 1829. Again, however, it was only in London, and it became the forerunner of the Metropolitan Police. The Bow Street Runners were absorbed into the London police force in 1839.

Local authority law enforcement goes back to ancient China, while in ancient Greece publicly owned slaves were used to maintain order. Policing in England, from 1700, relied on constables or 'watchmen' who patrolled the streets at night in various towns. In 1737, an Act of Parliament specified the number of constables/watchmen to be on the streets of London.

The first 'modern' police force was probably the French, established in 1667, who were also the first force in modern times to use horses (in the early eighteenth century) as part of their law enforcement duties. Subsequently, countries all over the world recognised the advantages of their officers working on horseback and maintain mounted police forces. In the UK today the mounted policeman is used for crowd control, especially at sporting events, as well as performing ceremonial duties. Worldwide mounted police forces provide an essential public service. Probably the best-known international mounted police force is the Royal Canadian Mounted Police, famous for their red jackets and brown hats.

Mounted police officer at Buckingham Palace.

Recreation

In the field of recreation, the horse has been a prime source of amusement from ancient to modern times. Chariot racing was a major sporting activity and was an event in the ancient Greek Olympics of 648 BC. Highly popular in Rome was the race along the Via del Corso, which involved riderless horses competing along perhaps the only straight road in the centre of the city. The race was first run in the fifteenth century and is the subject of several famous paintings. It was run annually for many years until finally in the eighteenth century a major rebuilding project made the road no longer suitable for the fast racing of uncontrolled horses.

Horse racing, often described as 'the sport of kings', has a long and distinguished history. It can be traced back to the twelfth century when knights returned from the Crusades. Its popularity increased from 1660 onwards, during the reign of Charles II.

All thoroughbreds can be traced back to three original horses: Byerley Turk (1680s), Darley Arabian (early 1700s) and Godolphin Arabian (1724–53). The formation of the Jockey Club in 1750 laid down the modern rules of racing, which are still followed today.

Steeplechase is another variant of racing and originated in Ireland in the eighteenth century when horses were raced from one church steeple to the next. The sport is now run under

The Race of the Riderless Horses, 1817. (Digital image courtesy of the Getty's Open Content Program)

National Hunt rules. Probably the most famous steeplechase is the Grand National, which is run every year at Aintree, Liverpool, and attended by around a quarter of a million racegoers.

Horses were also used during fox hunting. Fox hunting developed into an organised activity in the sixteenth century, primarily to put down foxes, which were seen as pests. The 'sport' continued until 2005 when it was banned in England, having already been banned in Scotland in 2002.

Equestrian events such as showjumping and dressage are mainly for professional riders who compete on a national and international level, as individuals or in a team.

Thousands of people also enjoy horse riding purely for pleasure, either on rented steeds or on their own horse.

The Liverpool and National Steeplechase at Aintree (1843) by William Tasker. (Yale Center for British Art, Paul Mellon Collection, B1981 25.7.64)

Travel

The industrial and commercial use of the horse was accompanied by developments in the carriage of people. Until the development of the horse-drawn tramway, railway and omnibus, if you did not own a horse yourself, you walked. More affluent members of society may have owned one or more horses to travel around locally, so taxes were levied on the numbers of horses and carriages owned. For long-distance travel the stagecoach offered reasonable comfort, but at a price.

Stagecoaches had existed for many years but were further developed in the seventeenth and eighteenth centuries as operators improved their speed. In 1750, the London to Cambridge route took two days, but by 1820 it was down to just seven hours. Coach owners also developed 'flying coaches' to run even faster, changing horses regularly to keep the average speed up. Four horses were the norm for coach travel. In 1754, this system enabled a coach to run from Liverpool to London in three days, and from Manchester to London in four and a half days.

Postal Service

The postal service, although expensive at the time, relied entirely on horses with single riders travelling from post to post, where at each one they exchanged letters for onwards transit. This system also employed 'flying' post horses.

Mail coaches began operating between all the major towns and cities of the UK, encouraged by a government impressed with the transit times achieved. Passengers were offered seats at a premium price. Mail coaches were usually accompanied by an armed guard.

Royal Mail coach. (Courtesy of the Post Office Museum)

Hansom cab for hire on a contemporary postcard.

Cabs

On offer to the wealthier citizen, who may not have owned their own horse and trap, was the horse-drawn cab. Cabs could be found available for hire, particularly in the main cities, such as London. They began in the seventeenth century but soon there were so many that they began creating traffic problems, so from 1652 a licensing system was introduced in London. This limited cabs for hire to 400 in the city, though was later increased to 700 in 1694, and finally abolished in 1832. Due to the congestion in Victorian London, the first traffic light was erected in 1868 on Parliament Square.

Cabs were two-wheeled and will be very familiar to TV and film followers of Sherlock Holmes. They had either open or closed fronts and the drivers worked very long hours in all weathers. Happily, in 1875 the Earl of Shaftesbury commissioned cabman's shelters to give London cabbies somewhere to rest their horses, stop for breakfast and shelter from the weather. By 1914 over sixty such shelters had been built, but today only thirteen remain as a reminder of the nineteenth-century horse-drawn cab.

Transport: Trams, Trains and Buses

Transport developed rapidly for the general public in the nineteenth century. Originally designed to move freight, trams were in evidence from the early days of the nineteenth century, and soon began carrying fare-paying passengers.

One of the first was the Swansea and Mumbles line, which opened in 1808. It was actually classified as a railway but in reality was originally a tramway. Its prime cargo was limestone but soon passengers were also carried. Others, including the Stockton and Darlington line (1825), forerunner of the synonymous railway, and the Gloucester and Cheltenham line (1809), were primarily built for freight but also carried passengers. Owners were always keen to explore new means to increase revenue.

Horse-drawn trams commenced in West Derby in 1880, and were replaced with electric trams in 1902.

The year 1814 saw the Oakeley open in Blaenau Ffestiniog as a narrow-gauge tramway to carry slate from the quarry to Portmadoc.

In 1860, Birkenhead citizens saw trams in their town for the first time. They were designed for passengers rather than freight and, similar to the Isle of Man tramway in Douglas, began operating in 1876. It still operates with horse-drawn carriages today as a tourist attraction.

The Stonehouse and Dartmouth line (1870) in Plymouth was the first tramway constructed under the new Tramways Act, its prime cargoes being granite and china clay. Opened in 1872, it was later converted to narrow gauge and electrified in 1901. The first trams used a pair of horses and an additional pair was required to negotiate the steep roads of Plymouth.

Trams first appeared in London in 1860, brought to the capital by the same man who introduced trams to Birkenhead, where he was in trouble and jailed for damaging the roadway. He also ran afoul of authority in London until tramlines were required to be set flush with the road. The trams were rapidly seen as a cheap form of transport for the

Horse-drawn tram, west Derby, *c.* 1900.

Four horses haul passengers in Plymouth up a steep incline. (David Voice)

average citizen and were soon deriving their main source of revenue from their human cargos.

Having been phased out by the mid-twentieth century, trams have now returned to our streets in cities such as Croydon, Gateshead, Manchester and Sheffield. Today they are seen as an efficient and cheap mode of transport with minimal impact on the environment. Other UK towns are also considering reintroducing trams.

The ordinary citizen was also soon the beneficiary of the horse-drawn omnibus. First seen on the streets of Paris in 1662, the concept was followed in other European cities before coming to Manchester in 1824 and London in 1829, and soon many towns up and down the country. The last horse-drawn omnibus ceased operating in 1911.

Summary

It is clear that the horse has played a major role in man's economic and personal development. The arrival of horse-drawn mass transit gave individuals opportunities to travel further to work and improve their individual income.

Although the horse has been used as a weapon of war over many years, it is in the commercial world that the horse, especially the heavy horse, has made the most impact, enabling increases in harvest yield and improving productivity across many industries.

During the industrialisation process in the late eighteenth and nineteenth centuries, horse power was a fundamental source of cheap power both on land and on water, and continued alongside the development of steam power.

With the exception of war and individual documented cases of ill treatment, man has treated his horse(s) with respect and care and a long-term bond has built up, ensuring the horse was well fed and watered and in turn proved to be a willing helpmate.

In the next two chapters the two major horse groups, the packhorse and the Shire, who together provided man with commercial freight services, are discussed.

3

The Packhorse

The term packhorse refers to a horse, mule, donkey or pony used to carry goods on its back or in side panniers. They were adept in difficult terrain and areas where roads were non-existent, preventing wheeled vehicles from operating. Until 1750 no wheeled vehicle could travel west of Keswick, so people relied on the packhorse for regular supplies.

The packhorse has been used from ancient times. It was used to carry freight in England from medieval times until the arrival of turnpike (toll) roads and the development of the inland waterways and canals in the eighteenth century. Elsewhere, they are still extensively used in developing countries and in certain military applications. Their main cargoes were salt, limestone, coal, fleeces and cloth. They also carried food, including fish and milk; in fact, a vast range of commodities were transported from the point of origin to the market for sale. Heavily used routes crossed the Pennines in northern England. There were also regular routes in Devon, the Peak District and radiating out from Sheffield.

The main breeds used were the Jaeger (derived from a German breed) and the Galloway, named after its origin in the Lowlands of Scotland.

A packhorse has distinctive characteristics and requires specific training. They need to be strong to carry heavy loads and tolerant of other animals in close proximity, noise, long ropes and the shifting of cargo when under load.

A laden packhorse could carry up to 400 lb (180 kg), dependant on the individual size of the horse, and frequently they comprised thirty to forty animals in one chain, looked after by a small workforce. More typically chains of twelve to twenty horses were run. They averaged around 25 miles (40 km) a day. The leader of the group carried a bell to warn other travellers of their approach.

There were few bridges on the routes, and those that existed were specifically built for the pack trains. The animals were rested at night when they were fed and watered. Many routes followed old Roman roads, and some were Viking in origin.

The village of Wycoller in Lancashire still has three packhorse bridges today. They were fairly roughly made and were built to accommodate a packhorse laden with side panniers. Bridges such as these frequently included passing points for travellers coming from the opposite direction. There are many old packhorse bridges throughout the UK that have survived.

Packhorse bridge in Wycoller, Lancashire. (Courtesy of *The Journal of Antiquities*)

In 1750, around 1,000 packhorses a day passed through Clitheroe on the Pennine route, and 200–300 loaded packhorses crossed the River Calder daily at a ford between Whalley and Clitheroe. The Pennine route was particularly important for trade, so gradually the main routes were improved, usually by laying stone setts. In bad weather the routes were especially difficult, making progress slow.

The UK economy was demanding better transport systems to service increasing trade, which the old packhorse method was not meeting. The gap began to be filled by the canal system, which was developed in the late eighteenth century. The Turnpike Act of 1773 encouraged private entrepreneurs to build metalled toll roads, which took business from the main packhorse routes, still leaving many challenging and difficult tracks. A leftover from this time are the many public houses named The Packhorse.

During the nineteenth century horses that transported military officers' baggage during campaigns were known as 'bathorses' from the French word *bat*, meaning 'packsaddle'.

In Pennsylvania, USA, in the 1790s, packhorses were used to haul coal from Summit Hill to cargo boats on the Lehigh River. During 1818–27, after completion of the Lehigh and Mauch Chunk canals, mule trains were used to return the 5-ton coal cars to the upper terminus. On the down leg the mules had the benefit of riding in the cars.

They were used extensively, either singly or in trains, by surveyors, fur trappers and gold prospectors due to the difficult terrain.

Native Americans used them to move from one area to another, as did traders, trading with local settlements.

In the nineteenth century huge packhorse trains operated on the Old Spanish Trail from Santa Fe, New Mexico, west to California.

Packhorses were found in many other countries too. In Japan they were used for personal transport. They were also used for freight carriage and to carry travellers' bags on a pack saddle, which varied in design from simple to elaborate. They also carried equipment and food for samurai warriors on military campaigns.

Today packhorses continue to provide an essential service, especially in North America and Australia where they are employed by hunters, campers, stockmen and cowboys to carry tools and equipment. They are also used by the United States Forest Service and the National Park Service to carry supplies as well as commercial goods to remote communities. In developing countries packhorses and donkeys take goods to market, carry supplies and do many of the jobs they have been performing for hundreds of years.

In modern warfare pack mules are used to bring in supplies where roads are poor and the fuel supply uncertain. Even more recently they provided a practical service to all sides of the conflict in Afghanistan.

Goyt Valley packhorse team.

4

The Draft and Shire Horse

Terminology of the Shire and draft horse is largely interchangeable in normal usage, but strictly speaking the Shire is a specific breed of draft horse. The draft horse is native to the English Midlands and has been described as descended from the English 'great horse', which carried men in full battle armour that could weigh up to 400 lbs. However, it is more widely assumed that the fighting horse is in fact descended from the destrier, which is more akin to the Andalusian or Friesian breeds. The nearest breed to the medieval fighting horse is probably the Percheron, now a threatened breed (see Chapter 2).

The draft horse (also known as draught or dray) is derived from the Old English *dragan*, meaning 'to draw' or 'haul'. It has also been called a carthorse, workhorse or heavy horse.

While there are a number of breeds they all share common characteristics, strength, patience and docile temperament, all of which made them ideal for heavy farm work.

In the late eighteenth century, selective breeding using imported mares from Holland improved the Shire. In 1853, the first Shire was imported into the USA and was followed by thousands of others, notably Shires from England and Clydesdales from Scotland, but also from other European countries.

The Percheron was America's favourite draft breed, with over 40,000 brood mares registered in 1918. A draft horse bred exclusively in America was the American Cream Draft. All draft horses needed to be strong workhorses, especially for work in agriculture.

Shire stallions are the largest breed of horse and can be over 17 hands high and weigh 2,000 lbs (*c.* 900 kg). The draft horse's metabolism is a little slower than riding horse breeds and therefore they need less feed per pound of body weight. Nonetheless, as a big horse it works its way through a significant amount of fodder per day – 1.5–3 per cent of their body weight – and can drink up to 21 gallons of water per day. Owners need to guard against overfeeding, which is usually not a problem with hardworking, heavy horses.

There are over thirty breeds of draft horse recognised today, the most popular for heavy work being the Shire, Clydesdale, Suffolk, Belgium and Percheron.

The Shire is recognised by its distinctive hair, known as feather, around the lower legs. There are various colours of Shire – bay, brown, black, grey or chestnut. In 1878, the Shire Horse Society was established in England and in 1885 the American Shire Horse Association was founded.

5

Social and Economic Life in Great Britain, 1800–1900

Life in Great Britain in the nineteenth century was one of massive contrasts. On the one hand the industrialisation and wealth creation in the country made a relatively few people very rich and they enjoyed all the benefits that money could provide for themselves and their families. On the other hand, the same process that generated many thousands of new jobs also ensured the majority of the population lived a life of drudgery and poverty.

The UK population in 1801 was just over 10.5 million, which grew by 3.5 times to 37 million in 1901, a period of 100 years. Similarly, the population of West Derby in 1825 was 500, rising to 1,873 in 1881, a 3.7 times increase in forty-eight years. The national rate of increase was at its fastest in the early years of the century, slowing down as the end of the century came into view. A significant factor in this growth was the average size of individual families. This, some have argued, was a direct result of the Poor Law legislation, which provided benefits to people of low income, especially those employed in agriculture. However, this theory did not square with families in Ireland and Scotland where poor relief was not obtainable, and yet larger families and population growth continued to rise. More likely factors were couples marrying at an earlier age and having children over a longer period, coupled with people living longer lives.

While it is accepted that life in Victorian Britain was tough, especially for the average worker, it was better and healthier than previous centuries. In spite of the rapid growth in new industries and resultant job opportunities, agriculture still remained the principal means of earning a living.

In 1851, agriculture employed 25 per cent of working men, as well as many women. Higher up the social scale, property owners and their lawyers derived a livelihood from their land, as did merchants selling farm produce either in bulk or through the numerous food markets throughout the country.

There was a concerted effort to increase the available cultivable land. For example, over 1,000 square miles of new land were added in East Anglia from drainage schemes. There was also an incentive to cultivate former wasteland into productive use, mainly as a result of the Napoleonic Wars (1803–15), which reduced international trade and therefore available supplies, particularly of food. The import of wheat became essential to ensure the population could be fed, although it was accompanied by major price rises, partly due to the Corn Laws, which were not repealed until 1846. All governments have found funding wars an expensive business, and throughout the nineteenth century hardly a year went by that Britain was not involved in a war somewhere in the world.

The cost of this policy was met by the population via taxation, not income tax but tax on goods, which accompanied higher prices. The average labourer carried a high burden: while the cost of food and other items rose, his income remained fairly static. As such, many relied on Poor Law benefits to keep above starvation levels. Prior to 1834 each parish was responsible for its own poor. This changed with the Poor Law Act of 1834, which made local unions responsible for poor relief, although in Liverpool it would be 1841 before an effective system was in operation. West Derby's system was up and running in 1837. In 1850, the average agricultural labourer earned £9 3*s* 2*d* per week, usually plus a tied cottage. The national wage was £19 12*s* 8*d* – over double the rural labourer's wage.

No wonder, therefore, that the workhouse was feared by many. Liverpool opened its first workhouse in 1732, with West Derby a year earlier in 1731. In 1832, there were 1,630 people in the local workhouses, rising to 1,773 in 1833, the cost being met by the parishes.

To illustrate the massive discrepancy in income by class, some landowners were earning in excess of £300,000 per annum, leaving vast fortunes to their descendants, while the average unskilled worker rubbed along on under £1,000 per annum. It was no surprise that the lower classes were increasingly resentful and that disorder occurred regularly throughout the century.

Many left the poverty of the land to move into better paid jobs in the growing towns and cities. Although West Derby itself remained a village, opportunities for new work existed in Liverpool and Lancashire. Cotton spinning and coal mining in Lancashire offered employment but at a cost of long days, six-day weeks and the continual danger of serious or even fatal accidents – it was long before the days of health and safety regulations.

A basic problem arose following the migration of people from rural areas to towns and cities, namely overcrowding. This, in turn, affected the general health of the poor, who were forced to live in overcrowded and unsanitary housing. In Ireland, the Potato Famine of the 1840s led to mass hunger and migration to England, adding to the overcrowding and health problems, especially on Merseyside.

Medicine and medical knowledge were advancing, but not quickly enough for the poor, as it still had to be paid for (see John Makin's doctor's bill, page 40).

Vaccination against smallpox became compulsory in 1853. Liverpool suffered cholera outbreaks in 1832, 1849, 1854 and 1866, while a national cholera epidemic broke out in 1848. There were a number of homespun and old wives' tales for the treatment of cholera.

The Public Health Acts of 1848 and 1875 led to significant improvements in general health. Hospital standards rose, not least due to earlier pioneering work by Florence Nightingale and others. Liverpool passed its own Act in 1846, the Liverpool Sanitation Act, which paved the way for the following appointments: Liverpool's first Medical Officer of Health, Dr William H. Duncan in 1847; James Newlands as Borough Engineer in 1847 at a salary of £700 per annum, plus a horse and a 'vehicle'; and Thomas Fresh, Inspector of Nuisances. These pioneering appointments collectively transformed

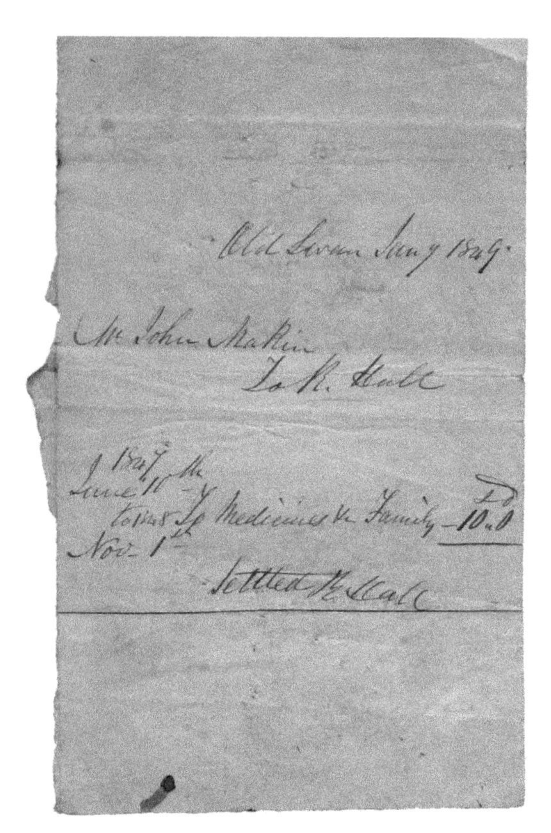

Old Swan Jany 1849

Mr John Makin
To R. Hall

1847
June 10th
to Nov 1st — To Visits & Medicines &c Family — 10.0

Settled R. Hall

Left: John Makin's medical bill by Dr Hall for his family's treatment – 10*s* was a substantial sum in 1849.

Below: Sir James Clark's prescription for treatment of cholera: '3 Drams of Camphor, 3 Drams of Laudanum, 3 Drams of Turpentine, 3 Drops Oil of Peppermint, a teaspoonful to be taken in a large glass of weak brandy and water for Dysentery. Brandy and water cold for Cholera a tablespoonful.'

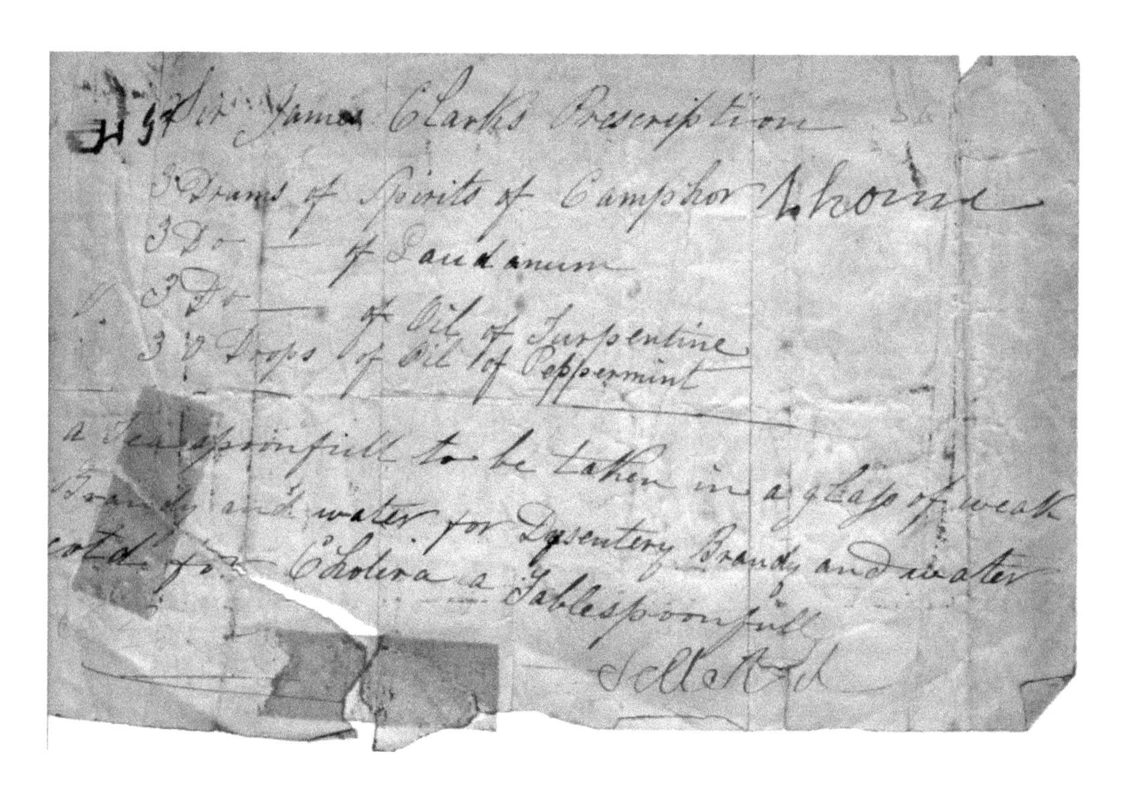

Sir James Clarks Prescription

3 Drams of Spirits of Camphor
3 Do of Laudanum
3 Do of Oil of Turpentine
3 Drops of Oil of Peppermint

a Teaspoonfull to be taken in a glass of weak Brandy and water for Dysentery Brandy and water cold for Cholera a Tablespoonfull

Receipt for Cholera
Half pint of the best Jamaica Rum
One pennyworth of Camphor
do " — " Spice Cloves
do " — " Laudanum

Bruise the Camphor before putting it into the bottle, then put the Cloves & Laudanum into the same bottle and shake it well for ten minutes & in two hours it will be fit for use
For an Adult take one tablespoonful in a wine glass filled with Cold water
For Children a teaspoonful

'Receipt for Cholera. Half pint of best Jamaican Rum. One pennyworth of camphor. One pennyworth of spice cloves. One pennyworth of Laudanum. Bruise the camphor before putting it in the bottle, then put the cloves and laudanum into the same and shake it for 10 minutes and in two hours it will be fit to use. For an adult take a tablespoon in a wine glass filled with cold water. For a child half a teaspoonful.'

Liverpool's health and environment. Dr Duncan's work was fundamental to improving the health of the citizens of Liverpool and is remembered by the city centre pub carrying his name.

James Newlands developed and built a major sewerage system for the city from 1848 to 1869 comprising almost 300 miles of main and subsidiary drains. The direct result of his work was that life expectancy in the city had doubled by 1870 from just nineteen in 1848. Naturally, word spread and the British government in 1855 asked Newlands if he could go to the Crimea to transfer his skills to that environment, resulting in high praise from Florence Nightingale herself.

The Great Stink of 1858, resulting from using the River Thames as an open sewer, was so bad that Parliament was forced to act and led directly to major improvements in sewerage disposal, not only in London but also in many other towns and cities.

Meanwhile, in Britain, encouraged by events in Europe where old regimes had been overthrown, democracy grew in strength and progressed throughout the century via the

A young girl entertains pub customers in Victorian Liverpool for pennies. (Copyright *Liverpool Echo*)

Reform Acts of 1832, 1867 and 1884, all of which extended the franchise, although it would be the mid-twentieth century before this was fully extended to women.

The rise of trade unionism towards the latter part of the century gave rise to hope that things could change. As a result of their action wages, which had been almost static, began to move upward and so the average worker enjoyed increased disposable income, giving the British economy a jolt in the arm as more money began circulating.

The rapid expansion of the railway system gave many the opportunity to travel further from home – to seek new work or even, for the favoured few, to go on holiday for the first time, although it would not be until 1938 that paid holidays for workers became law.

Trade increased, especially internationally, and more goods flowed into the country; as competition increased, prices fell to more affordable levels.

Accompanying these developments was a rapid increase in the availability of public entertainment. During the second half of the nineteenth century, numerous theatres and music halls opened and proved to be extremely popular.

Did John Makin take his wife and kids to see live entertainment? Although he worked hard and long hours, we know he had an income to be able to afford to take his family out. Liverpool carters enjoyed the music halls. By the latter part of the century, in Liverpool there were many places within reach of West Derby by the No. 9 tram. Makin may have taken the family to Cooke's Royal Amphitheatre of Arts, which opened in 1826 and provided circus, opera and theatre shows. It became the now famous Royal Court in 1881.

Alternatively, there was the Rotunda from 1863 or the Royal Colossium and Music Hall from 1850, which became the Grand Opera House in 1896. In fact, there were over forty places of entertainment to choose from in Liverpool. We can visualise the Makin family dressed in their best clothes and enjoying the latest production in a packed theatre with all the magic and colour of a live performance.

Above: Royal Court Theatre, Liverpool. Grade II listed. (Visit Liverpool.com)

Right: Rotunda Theatre, Scotland Road. (Copyright Ian Cowell)

As the century drew to a close all of the above factors coalesced, bringing benefits to all levels of society and a more even distribution of wealth, a process that had many years to go before the population felt they were starting to see some reward for their hard work. The nineteenth century saw massive and far-reaching changes across Britain as technological advances continued to develop and accelerate, as a more stable, healthier and generally wealthier and more confident Britain looked forward to the next century.

St George's Hall, 1900, with horse-drawn trams.

6

Liverpool Carters in the Nineteenth Century and Beyond

Liverpool's population grew rapidly during the nineteenth century, from 77,653 in 1801 to 684,958 in 1901 – almost ninefold in 100 years. A significant factor in this growth was emigration from Ireland from the 1840s onward. By 1850, 25 per cent of its population was Irish.

Although the growth of the railway network had vastly increased the volume and speed of moving goods to and from Liverpool and Birkenhead, increasing trade through the dock system, many of the docks were not directly linked to the railway system. Railways became well developed from the 1840s and there were links along Regent Road, colloquially known as 'the Dock Road'.

Throughout this period the dock system itself was being developed, notably by Jesse Hartley. Work commenced with Clarence Dock in 1830 and by 1859 it extended both northwards and south, eventually for over 7 miles, to meet the continued increasing demand for wharfside space.

As trade grew frequent bottlenecks arose, mostly on the quayside, calling for faster movement of goods to and from quays, wharves, warehouses and railway goods depots. This demand was filled for over 250 years primarily by the Liverpool carters.

Many of the dockside carters were provided by local transport companies or agents who supplied the carts, tack and horse with the carter as the loader/driver – an employed man. Some firms had several hundred horses each. A number were also employed by local firms who had daily business on the docks. A smaller number operated as sole traders, owning their own horse and cart, meeting all the food, stabling, farrier and veterinary costs directly from their earnings on the docks.

A variety of horses were used in Liverpool and the surrounding district. Shires were particularly valued because of their strength and long working lives, but other breeds of draft horse were common, dependant on the availability of the animal. Smaller horses were not excluded, even though they could only haul lighter loads. The owner operator provided the best animal he could within his income.

The horses were generally stabled as close as possible to work, and a number of stables were close to the dock system, from Bootle to Garston. Individual owners usually took their horse and cart home, ensuring the horse had suitable stable accommodation, with the cart left outside. Horses were generally looked after and well cared for; they were a valuable asset and it was in the owner's interest to keep them in good working health. There was even a horse that lived in Bootle and slept upstairs in the owner's home! The noise of the hooves clattering upstairs at night and again downstairs in the early morning would not have been welcomed by the neighbours (Ron Nixon, *Hilarious Memories of Bootle Beside the Sea*, 1987).

The work was hard and not particularly rewarding. Carters frequently started work at 05.30 a.m., getting the horse and cart hitched up and the horse fed. A fourteen–sixteen-hour day was common, and a six-day week was normal. Even as late as 1890 the *Liverpool Mercury* reported carters working fifteen–sixteen-hour days. The driver and horse worked in all weathers. If it was cold the horse would be covered with a thick blanket and the driver wore hobnail boots and muffled up with a scarf and his heaviest coat, usually tied around the waist with a piece of strong cord. On the quay the wind blowing off the river could cut through the heaviest of clothing and there was virtually no shelter. The Dockers' Umbrella (the Liverpool Overhead Railway), which provided a limited form of shelter from the worst of the weather, did not open until 1893.

In addition, carters faced other problems. The year 1867 had a particularly harsh winter and money was scarce, leading to random acts of violence. The *Liverpool Mercury* of 19 January 1867 reported that a carter with a load of coals was attacked and his cart overturned by a crowd of ruffians, and another carter was followed by a crowd who threatened to take his load of bags of flour.

The carter industry was controlled by licensing issued in Liverpool at 2*s* 6*d* per cart (1837). The cart had to have the owner's name painted on it in minimum 1-inch-high letters. There were numerous other regulations requiring how carts were positioned in the street and the driver's conduct (see Appendix IV).

Other trades supporting and essential to the smooth running of the carters' operation were blacksmiths, wheelwrights, suppliers of horse tack and fodder (forage) and farriers. Blacksmiths could repair damage to the iron fitments of the cart and re-rim a wheel, and many doubled up as farriers and also shod horses. This was normally the job of the farrier, and as shoes lasted a matter of only three to six weeks – they were in constant demand. Wheelwrights made and repaired the wooden carts, including the wheels. In nineteenth-century censuses some people described themselves as both a blacksmith and farrier, and even in some cases a vet as well. Until 1881 the RCVS could not prevent vets claiming the title without formal training.

The carts were normally four-wheeled and either flat bed or with small side boards – the specification formed part of the regulations. The wheels were wooden and fitted with iron rims. Haulage was by one-, two- and four-horse teams, dependant on the load. Loads carried were huge, 5–7 tonnes being typical for a single horse and 8–12 tonnes for a team.

Liverpool Corporation owned up to fifty horses. The role of these horses included everything from transporting mail, personnel and heavy loads around the city. The city had been persuaded to enter commercial transport by a local vet, Richard Reynolds, who advised the council that owning, breeding and operating their own horses was more efficient and cheaper than employing private contractors. The corporation's horses were stabled in Central Stables on Smithdown Road, which the council owned from 1858.

A select group of horses were also used to haul the city of Liverpool state coach on major civic occasions. Liverpool retained ownership of their own horses right up to 1960. The stables were finally sold for development in 1993. Not to be outdone, West Derby had its own ceremonial coach.

On both sides of the Mersey horses were employed continuously right through to the 1960s. At the peak there were over 20,000 horses working the streets of Liverpool – more than in any other city outside of London. The main source of employment was the docks in Liverpool, Birkenhead and Wallasey. Liverpool Corporation invested heavily in granite setts for road surfacing, which combined with special 'Liverpool horse shoes' that gave the horses a powerful grip. Young boys used to stand on street corners to watch sparks flying from the horses' hooves as they hauled the heavily loaded carts along the granite setts.

There was also gainful employment in the city's markets, where fruit and vegetables were sold daily in large quantities in and around Queen Square in the city centre. Carters transported the produce from the docks direct to the square, the fruit exchange in Victoria Street and to Paddy's Market in Cazneau Street.

West Derby lord mayor's coach, 1975. (Copyright Liverpool Records Office)

Double team. (Courtesy of Scottie Press)

Queens's Street fruit market. (Copyright Liverpool Records Office)

Emigrants being taken from their lodgings to RMS *Lucania*, *c.* 1895. (Copyright *Liverpool Echo*)

Although there was plenty of regular work for carters, getting a job for an individual driver was not easy. The larger firms such as Wm Harper, George Davies, JRT Transport and Jarvis Robinson had regular customers and therefore regular drivers; itinerant drivers were employed on a casual basis. The system required the driver to report at 7.30 a.m. to Carters' Corner, at the junction of Hopwood Street and Warwick Street, where they would hope to see a haulier's runner or foreman looking for extra drivers to cover sickness and holidays or a particularly busy spell. If the driver got a job, it was only for that day. Some lucky drivers obtained a number of consecutive days' work, and if they and their work was noted they might receive a permanent job.

The docks were the hub of most of the carters' work, and a great deal of the work was local. Major imports of cotton and tobacco from America were bread and butter for carters, who were also employed throughout the city collecting and delivering a wide range of products, including iron (there was a large ironworks in Sefton Street, backing onto Harrington Dock), coal and even furniture.

Long-distance traffic was the province of the packhorse until the growth of the railway network, but Liverpool carters were also employed working to and from Ormskirk, Rufford and Preston, frequently carrying to and from the dock system.

A side effect of so many horses operating in Liverpool was the volume of manure and urine they left on the city streets. A typical horse could deposit 20–35 lbs of manure and

2 pints of urine per day. This was not only unpleasant, but unsanitary. In London, the issue was called the Great Horse Manure crisis of 1894.

Liverpool was surrounded by farms and market gardens, where much of the manure from the city was sent. The enterprising Thomas Fresh (Inspector of Nuisances) also sent it to Formby and Freshfield, where the asparagus farmers, a speciality of the area, claimed it significantly improved their yield. In fact, it was Thomas Fresh's intervention that had led directly to the railway company building a new station named 'Freshfield' in recognition of him providing his own land for its construction, thus giving a new outlet for the disposal of manure. His motives were not entirely socially motivated though, as he wanted access to a railway station for his own benefit. However, as a direct result this area of Formby began to be known as Freshfield, and the name has remained to this day.

The carters were, for many years, an indispensable part of the local economy, contributing millions of pounds over the years. They realised how much the system relied on their hard work and believed if they were suitably organised they could improve their pay and conditions.

Trade unions were recognised by the law in 1824, but the idea was regarded with deep suspicion and organised labour was discouraged by employers. Moreover, as carters were frequently working alone and only got together either after work or during breaks in loading and unloading, organising them was not going to be easy.

Above: Plaque located in Formby dedicated to Thomas Fresh.

Left: Lunch on the Strand. (Streets of liverpool.co.uk)

Indeed, to become a member of a trade union in the first part of the century could be a dangerous activity. In 1834, aided by the Whig government, six agricultural labourers from Tolpuddle, Dorset, were arrested, tried, convicted and subsequently transported to Australia for signing a secret oath, but their real 'crime' was forming a trade union.

Carters had long regarded themselves a cut above the common labourer. They, with some justification, considered a man who could control a horse, look after it and ensure its continued good health, as well as working long days, had a saleable skill set.

Trade unions for workers developed from the 1830s. Robert Owen tried to set up a national trade union in 1834, but it collapsed. There were various other attempts during the 1830s and 1840s, largely under the Chartist banner, which was actually about the vote rather than workers' rights and conditions. Skilled trade unions followed in the 1850s and 1860s, but in the world of the Liverpool carter it was only towards the end of the century that they became properly organised as the Mersey Quay and Railway Carters Union, which was founded in 1889.

The organisers were particularly keen to promote the carter as a superior worker compared to the general labourer. It also attempted to restrict competition by charging an entrance fee of £2 to non-local residents, while Liverpool carters could join for 5*s* (25p today). There is no record of John Makin joining, though he lived outside the city.

Interestingly, this concept of restriction of competition survived on Liverpool docks right up to the container age, operated by the Liverpool branch of the T&GWU. It was rigorously enforced primarily by the trade union officers and their local officials (shop stewards) and was supported by the drivers' employers, being designed to deny new entrants so helping to keep haulage prices and therefore wages higher than they otherwise would have been.

The Carters' Union office was at No. 400 Scotland Road, a stone's throw from the docks. The Parrot Hotel, which still stands today, although sadly currently closed, is located at No. 347 Scotland Road on the corner with Hopwood Street, very close to Carters' Corner. It was a highly popular place of refreshment for both carters and locals alike for many years.

Membership to the union reached a peak of over 5,000 by 1910. Assuming half of the horses were in teams of two, this implies that only about half of the working carters were union members. Membership gradually declined in line with the fall in demand for horse-drawn carts.

Although Liverpool's workforce is often thought of as being highly militant, their union was actually noted for avoiding industrial action. An exception to this policy arose in 1911 with the Liverpool general transport strike, which the Carters' Union supported. This was one of the most significant strikes in British history and transformed trade unionism on Merseyside.

After the First World War, the Carters' Union accepted vehicle drivers as members and, in recognition, changed its name in 1920 to Liverpool and District Carters' and Motormen's Union. A very similar union had formed in Bolton in 1890, some nine years earlier, as the Bolton and District Carters' and Lorrymen's Union. Both unions, via various incarnations, were eventually absorbed into the T&GWU, which later became Unite.

A special event in the year of the Liverpool carters was the annual May Day parade, when drivers and horses were on show in all their finery to the enjoyment of residents. The horse itself was groomed from head to toe, and tails and manes were frequently plaited. The horse brasses were polished so they sparkled in the sunshine and the tack was also

Parrot pub, Scotland Road/ Hopwood Street, Liverpool – now closed and derelict.

given a good polish. The horse was usually covered in fresh flowers, while the cart was thoroughly cleaned and decorated with flowers from end to end. The carters themselves dressed in their best suits to accompany their horses, also looking their best.

Whole carters' families helped in the preparation of both horse and cart. George Wooding's three sisters, for example, prepared all the flowers for his horse Delightful. Once the parade started the colourful sight of numerous horses – many drawing traditional carts, others hauling brewers' drays or other forms of transport – was watched by crowds lining the whole route shouting encouragement.

This tradition was a colourful highlight in Liverpool for many years, much to the delight of the locals and especially the children. Happily, it continues to this day thanks to the surviving carters, the Liverpool Retired Carters' Association and the support of Liverpool museums.

Above left: George Wooding with Delightful.

Above right: Bass & Thwaites carts in Liverpool's May Day parade, 1976.

Below: Liverpool Corporation heavy horses in the May Day parade, 1910. (Liverpool Records Office)

7

West Derby from Earliest Times to 1900

The history of West Derby stretches right back to the Domesday Book (far earlier than Liverpool's). It was the largest area within the West Derby hundred (see Appendices I, II and III). A hundred was an administrative area that was subdivided into smaller units. The village of West Derby even had a castle to defend the area. This was built *c.* 1100 and was occupied by 140 foot soldiers, fifty bowmen and ten knights. Liverpool's own castle was constructed *c.* 1232 and effectively replaced West Derby as the regional stronghold. The occupants moved out of West Derby into the new Liverpool site and the old castle was abandoned and allowed to become derelict; by 1296 it was in ruins.

The West Derby hundred was huge, stretching from Meols in the north to Childwall in the south and from the Lancashire coast in the west to Leigh in the East – i.e., from the Ribble to the Mersey including all of present-day Liverpool, Southport and part of present Greater Manchester.

West Derby remained a village for hundreds of years, although it was larger than Liverpool for a long period, even after the demise of the castle.

The Middle Ages were a torrid time for England and most inhabitants. In West Derby and elsewhere the Black Death (1348–49) took a heavy toll – Walton cemetery was so full that a new burial ground was opened at St Nicholas' Church, Liverpool. In 1540, plague visited the area once more and killed almost 50 per cent of the population.

West Derby continued to suffer bad winters, failed harvests and appalling weather, although daily life went on and justice continued to be served. The Elizabethan courthouse (1586) indicated its importance as a centre of justice. This role was reinforced by the set of stocks mounted outside, which were in regular use into the Victorian period.

The rapid growth of the port of Liverpool quickly overtook the importance of West Derby and inevitably absorbed the area into the city, which was formalised under two legal Acts of 1835 and 1895. The area became a favourite place to live, and many fine new houses were built during the nineteenth century. Even today West Derby still has a village and countryside feel. It was this feeling of being in the countryside that attracted wealthier Liverpudlians to move to the area. An additional and perhaps more important factor was undoubtedly the less healthy environment in the city. The mortality rate for infectious diseases – smallpox, scarlatina (scarlet fever), typhus and measles – in West Derby was half that of adjoining Liverpool.

Until road improvements under the Turnpike Acts, communications with parishes and other areas outside West Derby remained very difficult. The adjoining district of Old Swan, named after the local pub the Three Swans, was only accessible on horseback or on foot until 1760 despite being on the main east–west packhorse route. Roads were no more than tracks, which even a cart found difficult to navigate. Early roads in West Derby were composed of sand, clay and outcrops of sandstone or where some granite setts had been laid down.

Matters improved with the Turnpike Trusts Act of 1725. This authorised repairs on the Liverpool to Prescot road. There were a number of sandstone quarries in the area, providing building materials and later long-lasting employment for John Makin in his role as carter as a proper local road system was constructed. In 1744, the Act was renewed for road extensions to be built. A third Turnpike Act was passed in 1752 authorising construction of the road from Prescot to Warrington, followed in 1760 by the surfacing of the road to accommodate carriages. But, of course, the turnpike roads had to be paid for. It would be the nineteenth century before better roads enabled rapid strides to be made in transportation.

At the turn of the nineteenth century West Derby remained a relatively poor village, even boosted by the new residents' additional wealth. In 1825, the population of West Derby was recorded as 500, which had risen to only 1,873 by 1881 – still a village, but an attractive place to live for many.

The first public transport in West Derby was horse-drawn trams, which served the area from the 1860s. The first tramway operating in the area was the Old Swan tramway, which commenced in 1861, but this was never a profitable enterprise and closed just a year later in 1862.

In 1860, George Francis Train, a controversial American entrepreneur who would later stand for election to be the American president, suggested to the Liverpool mayor a network of nine tramway routes that all radiated out from the Town Hall to a variety of destinations, including one to Fairfield and Old Swan and another to West Derby. The idea was to follow the existing omnibus routes and they would be hauled by teams of horses. The concept never got off the ground, so Train left for Birkenhead where he created what he claimed was the world's first tramline in 1860.

It would be Liverpool-based companies who were to provide West Derby with trams. In 1860, the Liverpool Road & Railway Omnibus Company was formed. In direct competition was the Liverpool Tramways Co. In 1871, the omnibus company changed its name to the Liverpool Omnibus & Tramways Company, and in 1875 merged with the Liverpool Tramways Company, now renamed the Liverpool United Tramways & Omnibus Company Ltd. By 1875 the company was operating 207 trams with a total of 2,894 horses and had 61 miles of track throughout the Liverpool area, including West Derby. In 1879, Liverpool Corporation purchased the company, leasing it back on 1 January 1880. The company was finally taken over in 1897 by the corporation, who immediately began a major electrification process of the entire network. The first electric tram began working in 1898 and the first West Derby electric tram appeared in 1900; electrification was complete by 1902. The last horse-drawn tram was finally withdrawn from service in Litherland, Liverpool, in 1903.

Horse trams survived in Ireland through to the 1960s, and they are still working even today on the Isle of Man. The electric trams, running over the same routes, effectively replaced the horse-drawn omnibus, only to be replaced themselves by motor buses after the Second World War.

8

A Famous Hotel, Murders and Ghosts, and Long-lost Trains

At Rainhill, a stone's throw away from West Derby, in October 1829, trials were held for locomotives to operate the new Liverpool to Manchester Railway. Stephenson's *Rocket* ultimately won, and the railway opened to a great fanfare in 1830. Although the line carried passengers, the owners had identified freight as being the main source of revenue for the line.

George Stephenson and *Rocket*.

The winter of 1830 in West Derby was particularly bad, leading to public disorder. The following year, 1831, saw a huge hailstorm, damaging hot houses in West Derby and presumably raising the cost of local produce. Over in Liverpool, tremendous rainstorms also caused significant damage.

The new nearby railway gave rise to some concern among the carters of both West Derby and neighbouring Liverpool regarding the future of their industry. Local carters soon had their concerns quelled as the main freight-carrying casualty of the early railway age was to be the packhorse, which could neither compete in terms of loads carried nor speed.

The sound of trains passing on the new Liverpool to Manchester Railway could be heard in West Derby and Old Swan, but it would be almost fifty years before trains arrived in West Derby itself. An important factor must have been the close proximity of the competing railway, which had stations at Huyton (originally Huyton Gate), Roby and Huyton Quarry. All three were opened in 1830 and were within easy reach of West Derby and Old Swan.

The Cheshire Lines Committee built an alternative line from Liverpool (Brunswick), as they were particularly keen to access the Liverpool docks, although Brunswick was not the ideal point of access. A later line from Liverpool Central completed the route to Manchester London Road station, which first opened in 1873. Subsequently, the Liverpool Extension line was built, branching off the Manchester line at Halewood and running through to Aintree. As part of this route stations were built at West Derby, Knotty Ash and Walton on the Hill – all opened in 1884.

The Cheshire Lines Committee (CLC) were not satisfied with progress and purchased additional land that enabled them to build a new station at Huskisson – a more suitable location to tap into the lucrative dock freight traffic. This enabled them to link the route into Huskisson from Fazakerley and Walton on the Hill in 1879 and develop Huskisson into a major goods operation. There was a complicated junction at Walton ('the Walton Triangle') to enable trains to access Huskisson from both the north and south.

Meanwhile, the company was building another extension from Aintree, which became the Southport & Cheshire Lines Extension Railway (SCLER). This ran from Aintree, out into the Lancashire countryside, then back over to the coast and finally into Southport Lord Street. It was completed in 1884.

The company had lofty ambitions for this part of its network. The terminus in Southport was a grand affair fronting the most important and fashionable street in the town. The company introduced a wide range of direct, long-distance services including one to London that carried a Pullman coach. The three stations immediately prior to Southport were located right on the coast and it was hoped they would attract wealthy holiday visitors.

Unfortunately, the dreams and aspirations of the CLC directors and shareholders were destined never to be fulfilled. Many of the stations located way out in the countryside were only accessible by horse and carriage, and even customers travelling by carriage or pony and trap had to be dropped off and collected on return.

Although small and hardly ever profitable, the Southport branch has a fascinating history, combining tragedy and at least one unique feature of 'railway mania'. A group of Manchester merchants funded the building of the luxurious Birkdale Palace Hotel via the Southport Hotel Company. It contained seventy-five rooms and spacious conference

West Derby station in the 1950s and after closure.

Lord Street station, Southport. (disusedstations.org.uk)

facilities and was set very close to the beach at Birkdale in no less than 20 acres of grounds and gardens. It opened in 1866 at a cost of £60,000. The promoters had planned for an exclusive location with every facility to pamper their guests. This ambition was achieved and for many years the Birkdale Palace was the largest and most luxurious hotel not only in the Southport area, but also in north-west England.

Visitors began arriving, typically by carriage or on horseback. The hotel boasted a coach house for theirs and their client's carriages and stables for the horses. Crucially, however, the promoters' business plan failed to allow for the fact that there was no proper road access, omnibus train or tram route to it, which severely limited access for customers; unsurprisingly, this had a detrimental effect on visitor numbers. Sadly, it went into liquidation after a number of lean business years.

The new owners completed a total refurbishment in 1881, reducing the extensive grounds to a more manageable 5 acres. In 1884, salvation was thought to have arrived in the form of the Cheshire Lines Railway's Southport extension, who built Birkdale Palace station right alongside the hotel. The hotel was further modernised with new baths, direct salt seawater and a lift. It reopened with sixty members of staff as a hydropathical spa to rival successful Victorian hydros elsewhere, and was also marketed as an ideal recuperation facility for customers following illness.

The grounds provided sports facilities for tennis, croquet, bowling and archery. There was also a children's playground, bowers, walks and seating. A high embankment on the seafront shielded customers from the wind and it was topped off with a 650-foot

Birkdale Palace Hotel and grounds, 1940s. (Copyright *Southport Visitor*)

promenade. Inside was equally luxurious, having a classy restaurant, superb ballroom and no fewer than three bars.

By 1919 electricity had been installed throughout the building, which was powered by a steam-driven generator. Each upgrade increased the hotel's capacity, which now offered 200 bedrooms and suites.

A direct rail connection enabled customers to walk directly from their train into the hotel's reception. No longer did you have to bring your own horse and carriage. As an added bonus, the bright lights, cafés, restaurants and all manner of entertainment were only one train stop away in Southport. What more could the discerning and well-off clients want or need?

Unfortunately, shortly after the original opening the Birkdale Palace Hotel was subject to rumours of disaster and ghosts. It was suggested that the hotel had been built the wrong way round with the 'wrong side' facing the sea. Allegedly, this was blamed on the architect, William Mangall, a partner in the Manchester-based architectural partnership of Mangall and Littlewood, who as a result of the criticism was said to have jumped off the roof of the newly built hotel to his death. Subsequently, his ghost was said to regularly travel in the lift to the top floor – despite the lift having been installed many years later. The ghost was reported to be seen or heard on the spot on the top floor where he was presumed to have jumped from. The original plans for the hotel, now in the custody of Southport's authorities, do in fact show the hotel facing west and not east as built. What is certain, however, is that William Mangall died in his bed of consumption in 1868. His son died by suicide, though, so he may well be the source of the story.

But no one could have foreseen the tragedy of 1886, which was played out in almost full view of the hotel's guests and staff. It was another ordinary day on 8 December 1886, followed by a cold and dark midwinter evening. Many people were starting to think of Christmas, which was just over two weeks away. The shops on Lord Street were well stocked for the forthcoming season and Christmas trees and twinkling fairy lights were everywhere. People were feeling jolly as they shopped for Christmas and the children's presents.

Just a short distance from Lord Street, at the Birkdale Palace Hotel, the forthcoming festivities were eagerly anticipated by visitors and staff alike. The hotel's public rooms were all gaily decorated for Christmas and New Year as the staff prepared for a busy period. The head chef was particularly busy, ensuring his orders were sufficient for the hotel's guests over the festive season.

And yet there was something different about that evening. The sky seemed darker than normal, and just before nightfall the wind started to increase. By evening a full-blown storm arrived at the coast; the wind howled as it began to reach gale force. The hotel felt the full force of the wind, which rattled the windows as it roared in from the west unopposed across the raging sea and the empty beach outside. What few knew at the time was that a deep depression had crossed Northern Ireland at around 2 p.m. that day. The barometer fell rapidly, and it was later revealed that the depression was the deepest ever recorded.

On 5 December, three days earlier, the three-masted, iron-hulled 400-ton sailing barque *Mexico* was in Liverpool docks and had just completed loading a mixed cargo, much of it having been brought to the ship's side by the ever-busy Liverpool carters. The ship had been built in Sunderland in 1860 and after several changes of hands was now owned by a German company, Oetling Gebruder, of Hamburg. The master and crew of twelve had said their goodbyes to loved ones and the vessel quietly slipped her moorings and sailed out of Liverpool docks on the ebbing tide, bound for the faraway port of Guayaquil in Ecuador, over 6,000 nautical miles and many weeks of sailing from Liverpool.

On the evening of the 8th a mayoral ball was in full swing in Southport's popular Cambridge Hall. As the happy partygoers enjoyed the music and dancing late into the evening the revelry was suddenly interrupted by the loud boom of the lifeboat gun, which was the signal of what was to become the worst lifeboat disaster ever. The *Mexico* had sailed directly into the teeth of a west–north-west gale. The ship had dropped anchor off the Birkdale coast in an attempt to seek shelter, but had dragged it and was being driven aground between Ainsdale and Birkdale by the sheer force of the wind, which had now worsened with heavy rain and snow showers. The ship was soon firmly aground just off the coast, and both ship and crew were in grave danger.

Mexico aground off Birkdale.

The master had signalled for aid and the Southport lifeboat, *Eliza Fernley*, with a crew of sixteen, launched at around 11 p.m. Shortly afterwards the St Anne's lifeboat, *Laura Janet*, with a crew of thirteen, also launched and both headed for the two red lights displayed on the mast of the stricken vessel.

Although neither boat actually reached the *Mexico*, the *Eliza Fernley* was close enough for a lifeboatman to get ready to throw a line. At that very second a huge wave swung the lifeboat broadside and a mountain of water lifted the boat clean out of the raging sea, turning it over with the crew trapped underneath. The lifeboat was expected to self-right but failed to do so and although four members of the lifeboat crew managed to get themselves from underneath and cling to the keel, only two survived the ordeal. Fourteen of the sixteen-man crew were lost. The *Laura Janet* simply disappeared – lost with all thirteen hands. The boat was found around noon the following day opposite the Birkdale Palace Hotel without sails and mast, which were later recovered off Spencer's Bank.

Meanwhile, a third lifeboat, the *Charles Biggs*, had also launched from its base at Lytham – its maiden launch. It reached the *Mexico* and rescued all twelve crew, who had lashed themselves to the ship's rigging while awaiting rescue.

A total of twenty-seven lives had been lost on that wild night, leaving sixteen widows and fifty children without fathers. The grim task of recovering the bodies took place the following day and the Birkdale Palace coach house was used as a temporary morgue for fourteen of the drowned men. A hastily convened coroner's enquiry was held in the hotel and the jury viewed the bodies in the coach house.

The Birkdale Palace's coach house was later converted into a pub, primarily to keep the general public out of the hotel's more exclusive bars. The pub was later renamed the Fishermen's Rest in memory of the lives lost in 1886, which is particularly appropriate as all the lifeboat crew members were fishermen by trade.

The pub is reputed to be haunted by the spirits of the dead men. There are also reports that the pub is haunted by a little girl who moves objects around at night. On the anniversary of the tragedy a reading of a poem takes place followed by a minute's silence. As a further tribute to the men lost, the bar's handrail includes a series of fourteen brass mermaids.

Naturally, with such loss of life national public concern ensured a relief fund was launched. It was believed to be the first national appeal and thousands of pounds were raised for the benefit of the lost men's families, including contributions from both Queen Victoria and the German emperor.

The wreck of the *Mexico* was sold for £45 to a Preston firm who had it re-floated, towed to Preston and repaired. The ship then went on show off Lytham Pier for two years. It was then sold again and sent on an 8,000-mile voyage to the Falkland Islands, from which it safely returned only to run aground again off the Scottish coast at Tantallon in 1890. This time there was to be no re-floating and it was declared a total loss, so the ship ended its life in home waters not far from where she was built.

Four memorials to the disaster were later erected – one in St Anne's, two in Southport and one at Lytham. The disaster also featured in a BBC documentary in 2005.

Southport memorial to lifeboat men lost in the *Mexico* disaster.

The Birkdale Palace Hotel continued to welcome and serve customers, but over the years its reputation of being haunted gained traction, with numerous stories of ghosts appearing in the massive building.

The railway alongside was closed from 1917 to 1919 as a war economy measure, which had some impact on visitors, but by 1919 trade was once again brisk and the owners launched a direct air service from Blackpool Airport to their own landing area alongside the hotel. Visitors were now arriving by aircraft, car and train.

The Second World War began in September 1939 and the hotel continued to do good business. In 1942, the government requisitioned the building and handed over the hotel to the Red Cross, who used it for the recuperation of US aircrew, particularly bomber crews. Over 15,000 thousand aircrew passed through the hotel, and in some cases met their future wives among the hotel staff.

The years post-war saw a strong revival in hotel bookings nationwide, and the Palace enjoyed its fair share too. The 1950s and early 1960s were probably its best years, with many famous people staying. Frank Sinatra was a guest in 1953 while performing for five nights at the Liverpool Empire. Other guests included Clark Gable, Peter Sellers and Judy Garland, who was remembered for her lavish parties held in the ballroom. Even the Beatles played the Palace in 1962. The hotel was also the base for the Hungarian football squad and their staff during the 1966 World Cup.

Although the hotel had done good business in the 1950 and 1960s (even the loss of the rail link in 1952 seemed of little consequence at first), its paranormal past, always in the background, was now to become the major factor dominating the hotel's reputation. The dark side always seemed to come to the fore in the history of the Palace: there had been a double suicide of two sisters; a total of eleven murders had been committed in the hotel over the years; and in 1961 a six-year-old girl, Amanda Jane Graham, was kidnapped by a hotel night porter later named as Alan Victor Wills, and her body was discovered under the bed in his room.

Wills was convicted of the murder and sentenced to life imprisonment. He was aged thirty-three, but at his trial he was described as having a mental age of eleven. All the grisly deaths added to the rumours and alleged sightings of ghosts, especially female ghosts. The film *The Haunted House of Horror* (1967) was shot there – the producers had turned down the chance to book the then unknown David Bowie to appear in the film, using the American actor Frankie Avalon instead. Norman Wisdom starred in the film *What's Good for the Goose* (1969) and the hotel itself featured in the film. By 1967 the writing was on the wall for the hotel, in spite of the many famous guests it attracted, as it was rapidly running out of cash. The then owners, Heddon Hotels, went into liquidation and the business was wound up. In fact, the Norman Wisdom film was the last big event to take place there.

In 1968/9, the hotel was used as a production base for films by Tigon British Film Productions, owned and run by producer Tony Tenser. Samuel Anthony Tenser was a larger-than-life character who famously lost an opportunity in 1963 to book the Beatles to appear in a film he was producing in London because he refused to pay their rail fares from Liverpool. Tony knew everyone worth knowing in show business and was probably the nearest Britain got to a Hollywood-style film mogul. He claimed to have coined the phrase 'sex kitten' for Bridget Bardot and gave Roman Polanski his first two English films as a director.

Having been in film production for many years and having used the Palace for filming, he recognised the potential of the huge building and its location and set about trying to save the old building. He proposed his company and Southport Council jointly buy the hotel to run it as a film studio. The council refused to enter into a commercial venture and the opportunity was lost. Whether the type of films Tony was mainly associated with – known in the business as 'sexploitation' – had any bearing on the council's decision has not been recorded.

Tony went back to his London base and continued filmmaking until his retirement in 1974. In 1978, he returned to Southport with a new wife, living in the town until his death in a care home opposite his old house in 2007. His death occurred on 5 December – exactly 121 years to the day the *Mexico* had sailed from Liverpool on that fateful voyage.

The hotel lay empty for a while until it was sold for demolition and redevelopment of modern housing. A demolition team arrived in 1969 from Rochdale, a no-nonsense gang of men led by their foreman Joseph Smith, who had orders to demolish building and leave only the coach house remaining. But the hotel was not going down without a fight. As soon as the demolition team arrived the lift began to travel up and down the five floors on its own, even opening and closing the doors as it stopped erratically at various floors, in spite of the fact the electricity supply had been disconnected. The demolition team were genuinely frightened, and it took all of the diplomacy of their foreman to keep them focused on their work. To save expenses the bosses of the demolition team had arranged to house their workers in the hotel itself. Having to sleep in the hotel only added to their fears. Indeed, at times they said they were locked in their own rooms by a mysterious force.

Eventually they attacked the lift, by now residing on the third floor, with massive hammers until finally it broke free from whatever was holding it. It fell down the lift shaft, burying itself in the basement with an enormous crash. The ghost lift remains part of Birkdale folklore to this day.

Other stories from the demolition team included hearing a man and woman arguing, firstly on the top floor and then later in reception, even though that area was impassable due to rubble. They also heard the unmistakable sound of high heels in the lobby. The local police also received a call said to be from the hotel by a woman claiming to be locked in one of the rooms. On arrival at the hotel, they did not find anyone in distress but discovered the phone lines had all been disconnected. And the story does not end there.

It is possible to explain some of the events logically. For example, local residents said that courting couples took advantage of the empty rooms. Could they be the source of the voices heard? Had the demolition team made up some of the stories of locked rooms in an attempt to be put in better accommodation elsewhere? But the fact remains that the building was over a hundred years old and had seen many tragedies over those years, so maybe, just maybe, there were indeed paranormal happenings that logic cannot explain.

In 1897, the Lancashire and Yorkshire took over the SCLER, which became part of the Liverpool Southport and Preston Junction route. Way out in the Lancashire countryside were the remote stations of Altcar and Hillhouse and Barton. The L&Y introduced a unique feature on this part of the route, known as the 'Altcar Bob'. This was a one-coach train running between Altcar and Southport from 1907 to 1938, but it sometimes terminated at Barton. The coach was pulled by a tiny tank engine designed so it could operate without turning – it had an extra set of controls in the rear to do so. The origin of the name is lost to the mists of time. Some people claim it was named after a well-known regular driver called Bob, others that it was named after the cost of the fare being 1*s* (5p), known in slang as a 'bob'.

The service was largely designed for local passengers. In addition to the regular stations there were designated halts with no services or platforms. In the hours of darkness prospective passengers would strike matches to signal to the driver they needed picking up. The train had its own steps to facilitate this unusual method of uplift and drop-off.

The Cheshire Lines Railway from Liverpool to Manchester and the Southport branch was never a great success. In fact, no fewer than four competing lines had been constructed offering services between Liverpool and Manchester. The Liverpool Extension and the Southport CLR was too long (over 30 miles) and therefore too slow to compete either with the original line and the later Lancashire & Yorkshire Railway's more direct (18 miles) Liverpool to Southport line. The journey from Liverpool Central to Southport Lord Street was typically ninety minutes, with competitor L&Y being about an hour.

The Southport section became part of the new nationalised British Railways in 1948, but dwindling traffic brought about closure from Aintree to Southport in 1952. The splendid Victorian terminus in Lord Street firstly became a bus depot, then a supermarket and now is a budget hotel. The bus station is remembered in the building's name – now the Ribble Building – and the Cheshire Lines insignia remains on the station clock. The route from Woodvale to Southport is now the Coastal Road and the remainder of the route is part of the Pennine Trail and a cycle trail.

The passenger route from Liverpool Central to Aintree closed progressively between 1960 and 1972. West Derby station was closed to passengers in the late 1960s and to freight in 1976, and many of the other stations on this part of the route closed over a similar time frame. The company had originally purchased enough land to build four tracks, but only ever built two; however, much of the original CLC route remains. The stations in Widnes, Warrington and Urmston are virtually original. Some of the old stations form part of the Merseyrail Loop Line, and even Liverpool Central station survives underground.

The ideas men, planners and the promoters of the Cheshire Lines Committee must have felt bitterly disappointed at the slow demise of their railway. It promised so much in the early days. Two direct dock connections were created at Brunswick and Husskisson. Trade through the Liverpool dock system in the late nineteenth century was massive and continued to grow during and after the First World War. They had linked the two boom cities of the century, Liverpool and Manchester. International trade was rapidly becoming global and the CLC felt well placed to benefit from this growth.

The Liverpool and Southport extensions were seen as natural additions to the network, joining many communities to the system and having the added advantage of linking Manchester and Liverpool to the new holiday market of the North West. Aintree also had direct access to the famous racecourse, with excellent station facilities throughout and a system ripe for profitable growth over many years.

The north-west section was part of a huge railway system and a large company with substantial resources. But the business decisions were almost always behind the competition, and after nationalisation in 1948 much of the network was already doomed – long before Dr Beeching with his notorious programme of savage cuts arrived.

9

John Makin and His Family

Liverpool carter John Makin was born in Roby-with-Huyton, Lancashire, on 13 November 1803. His father and mother were William and Lydia Makin, both aged twenty-seven at the time of John's birth. He was christened in St Michael's Church, Huyton-with-Roby, on 11 December 1803.

The area is an ancient one. Huyton is mentioned in the Domesday Book of 1086 where it is spelt 'Hitune', meaning High Town, and formed part of the West Derby hundred. Earlier, around the seventh century, the area had been settled by Angles.

The township is located at the edge of what was the Lancashire coalfield, and in the nineteenth century Welsh coal miners settled there to work in them. A Nonconformist chapel was built for them close to Huyton Quarry.

Quarrying was an important source of employment, both for quarrymen and carters. The Cronton Coal Colliery continued in operation until 1984. Over the years the area also had a pottery, an ironworks, a gasworks, rope works, blue works, an electric lamp works and later a chair-making factory. During the industrialisation process of the nineteenth century short streets of terraced houses were built to accommodate the workforce.

St Michael's Church is an ancient seat of worship and possibly dates back to Saxon times, but certainly a church stood on the site in the twelfth century. The present building is medieval in origin, although has been significantly altered in later years, and is Grade II listed.

We know little of John's early years but can assume he had the benefit of a basic education. This would possibly have been in a local Sunday school, although there was a free school in West Derby from 1677. There was also Old Swan Charity School (built in 1792) and a grammar school in Huyton from at least the sixteenth century. He may have attended any of these institutions. Until 1874 all education was privately funded and paid for by the pupil's parents or philanthropists. We know from his workbooks that he had been taught copperplate writing and could clearly read well. We also know he was married at twenty-one and his first child, Thomas, was born in 1828, so he probably left whatever education he was receiving by the age of fourteen.

He married Catherine Case on 4 September 1825 in St Mary's Church, the parish church of Walton on the Hill – not to be confused with St Mary's in West Derby. By then he had

Left: St Mary's Church, Walton-on-the-Hill.

Below: St Michael's Parish Church, Huyton.

left Huyton and moved to West Derby, where he and Catherine set up home. Catherine was three years younger (born 1806) than John and was nineteen at the time of their marriage.

Both churches are built of local sandstone, as is the much later Liverpool Cathedral along with many other local buildings and places of worship. St Mary's has had a more dramatic history than St Michael's. A church on the site was mentioned in the Domesday Book, but that was rebuilt in the fourteenth century and significant alterations were made to the fabric in the eighteenth and nineteenth centuries. Sadly, the church was destroyed (apart from the tower) in the Blitz during May 1941. It was rebuilt between 1947 and 1953 to the original exterior design but with a new interior. It is also Grade II listed.

John and Catherine had four children together over the next twenty years: Thomas (1828), William (1830), Catherine (1843) and Anne (1845). In the 1851 census all the family were living at the same address, and if John had hoped one or both of his sons would join the family business this was not to be, as Thomas' occupation was entered as gardener and William, a labourer. However, his youngest, Anne, married William Rogers from Flint on 13 August 1874, who was a wheelwright – a maker and repairer of cart wheels. They lived at No. 48 Lord Nelson, then moved to Shaftesbury Terrace and finally to No. 165 Prescot Road. They had one daughter, Margaret, who became a school teacher, which would have restricted her own marriage plans.

John was a local carter, owning his own horse and cart. He lived in Grey Horse, West Derby, an area that no longer appears on any local maps. It lay between West Derby, Knotty Ash and Old Swan, and comprised a number of workers' cottages.

In one of his workbooks he describes his address as 'Grey Horse, Knotty Ash near Liverpool'. His veterinarian alternatively describes the same address as 'Near Old Swan', whereas his tax collector addresses his correspondence to 'Prescot Road'. The cottages were very near Prescot Road and were primarily occupied by working-class families. In the church records a number of people gave Grey Horse as their address over the years and references continue until 1907. Jobs of those living there include gardeners, blacksmiths, painters, carters, brewer, brewer's carters, coachmen and wheelwrights.

There was, and still is, a Black Horse Lane, which lies between West Derby and Old Swan and today is on the No. 9 bus route. We know that John Makin hauled rock and stone to Black Horse Lane, possibly for its construction or upgrade.

There is a record of a baptism in the church of St John the Evangelist in Knotty Ash – Sarah Platt of No. 12 Black Horse Lane – on 3 January 1912, whose father Edward was described as a 'pavior' (a person who laid cobblestones). The church was built in 1834/36 by Richard and Paul Barker of Huyton, who were local businessmen and owned several quarries and a large underground icehouse. They were brickmakers and owned other local enterprises and built a number of local buildings. No doubt much of the sandstone used locally came from their quarries. In digging one of their quarries they created the cellar for the Joseph Jones Brewery in Knotty Ash. The brickworks also provided regular haulage business for John Makin, and there are many references in his workbooks to carting from Barkers Brickworks.

There is another surviving location from the eighteenth century under the delightful name of Little Bongs. The origin of the name is shrouded in mystery but may have come

Little Bongs. (Courtesy of David Harrison)

A Knotty Ash brewery staff outing, *c.* 1920. People can be seen looking out from the first-floor windows. (Copyright Liverpool Records Office)

from the wooden 'bungs' hammered into barrels of beer. The cottages were occupied by people from similar economic backgrounds as those living in Grey Horse and the photo here gives a flavour of working-class accommodation at the time. Little Bongs is opposite Springfield Park and is approached via an archway.

Once settled in Knotty Ash/West Derby, John remained there for the rest of his life. In the 1881 census, by which time he was likely retired, he was recorded as living at No. 47 Lord Nelson, next door to his daughter Anne, her husband William and their daughter Margaret.

He would almost certainly have kept his horse very close to home, probably in a stable with the cart alongside. There were a number of open public spaces on which the horse could graze, and the horses from the trams also enjoyed grazing and a rest from pulling a heavily laden tram.

Makin's work was primarily in the immediate neighbourhood, although he had many trips to Liverpool and other locations within a 10-mile radius.

The images here give an impression of the area in the nineteenth century. The area remained very much a rural village with little housing. Housing was mixed and consisted of rows of small terraced housing for workers and their families and large, purpose-built, grand houses for the wealthier residents.

Much of West Derby was devoted to farming, and there were four mills in the immediate area: a watermill in Castle Street, a nearby horse mill, one in Mill Lane and one in the north-east of West Derby – Ackers Mill (Ackers was a large local farm). There was strong demand from farmers for local mills to grind their corn and produce flour for sale in the immediate neighbourhood and Liverpool.

Seventeenth-century cottages – Knotty Ash painting.

Industrial activity in the area of Old Swan included a flat glass factory started by Frenchmen in 1825 who had the technical knowledge to make clear and flat glass as opposed to the bull's-eye style then in widespread use. Forty Frenchmen came to start up the operation and teach local labour the techniques. The business became highly successful. Sheet glass for the Liverpool Custom House was sold at 9 and half pence per foot, and plate glass for the original Royal Insurance Building was sold at 7*s* 6*d* per foot – fancy prices for the times. The business was so cash rich it was able to afford to pay its workforce £3 10*s* per week – virtually double the local going rate. Sadly, after a number of successful years the business closed, mired in a fraud case, and was subsequently purchased by Chance Bros and Pilkington's. Gascoigne Cottages and The Glass House pub are reminders today of the French influence.

The other main local industrial process was the ropeworks, which produced on two local sites, rope being in huge demand in the port of Liverpool. St Oswald's Street was the prime site. The business was started in 1838 by Garnock Bibby & Co. The partners, having served at sea themselves, recognised that the quality of ropes used on a ship could mean the difference between life and death to the sailors, so they produced top-quality ropes and were renowned for the standard of their work.

With a number of local industries in the immediate area and the demands from the agricultural business all needing local haulage, there was certainly enough work to keep John and his fellow carters busy for the present and many years ahead.

His primary cargoes were bricks, stones and straw. The bricks and stones were mainly hauled from local quarries and brickworks, while the straw and hay were carried on behalf of farmers. John therefore had quite a range of customers all-year round, including local authorities as well as individual business owners. In view of the variety of cargo carried and the basic nature of many of them, we can assume that the cart was equipped with side boards to keep it all safe while in transit (see Appendix IV for regulations on carts).

Oddly, in Australia at the time carters were known as 'draymen', a term in England reserved for beer carters. The Australian cart, or dray, was a flat cart with short side boards, equipped therefore to carry a range of cargo and similar to its counterpart in England.

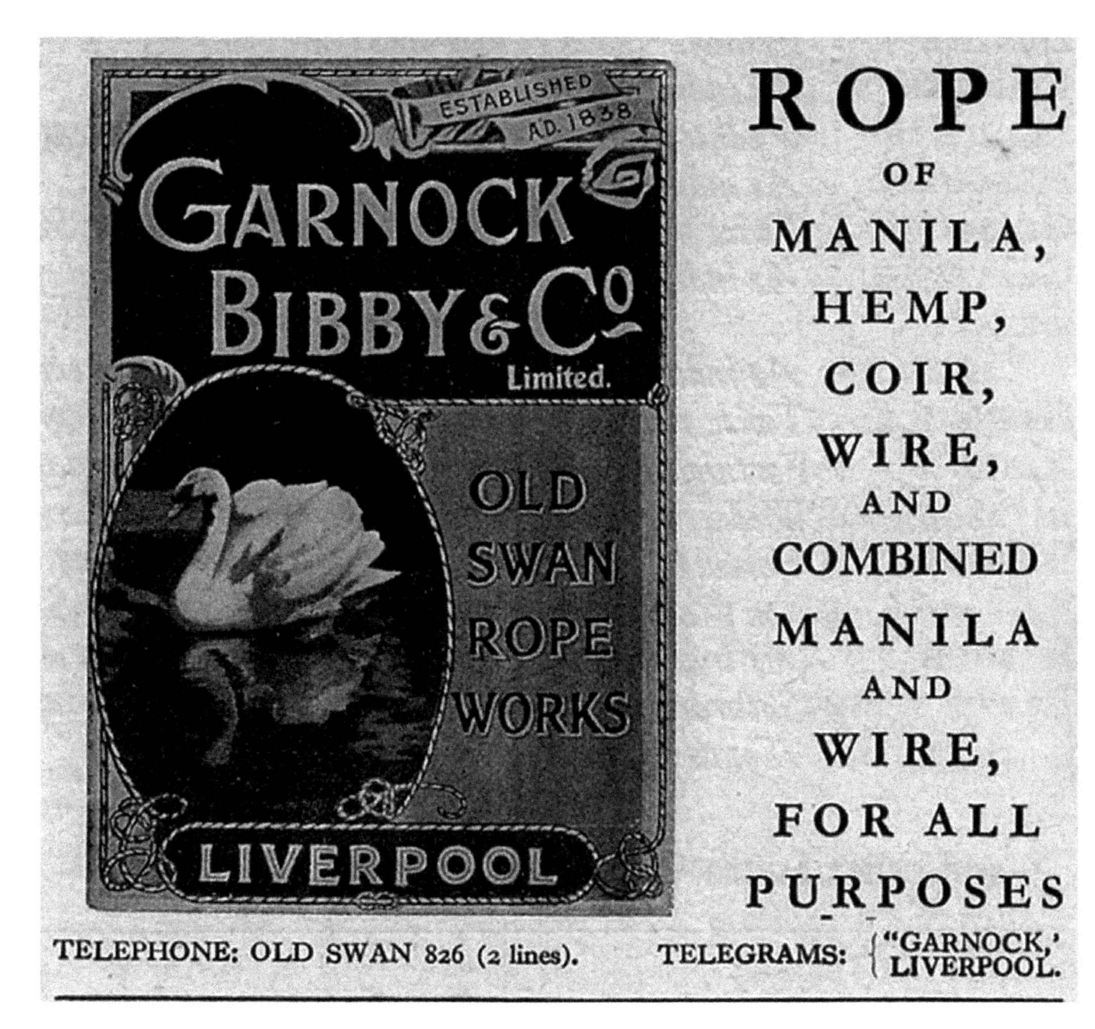

Advertisement for Liverpool Rope Works. (Grace's Guide to British Industrial History)

10

John Makin's Workbooks

His Life and Work

John's original workbooks provide a wealth of information on the work carried out, the charges made and the customers he worked for. The dates of the books are:

Book 1 – June 1857 to July 1857
Book 2 – March 1862 to October 1862
Book 3 – 1 September 1864 to early 1867

The records are spread over nine years, although few are in complete detail as they are clearly working books carried in the owner's pocket, so subject to considerable daily wear and tear. There are also numerous side notes unrelated to work. For example, in one book he has written the names and dates of the births of his children – perhaps he was a bit bored while waiting to load or unload.

He also notes payments received by the amount and date. And, typical of the period, extended credit was endemic. He seems to have hired himself and the rig out by the day and his standard rate throughout the records appears to have been 6–7*s* (30/35p in today's money) per day. The number of daily loads varied, but not the price. The records are frequently out of sequence – probably to keep individual accounts for each client.

Book 1

Looking at some of the entries in the oldest book, we can see a pattern of working a six-day week. There was also a dependence on a handful of customers and a heavy reliance on hauling bricks.

In June 1857, he carted one load of barley and hay on behalf of Mr Leonard Farthing, charged at 6*s*.

From 1–18 June, on behalf of Mr Mersey and himself, he hauled seventeen loads of bricks. There is no note in the book of the charges.

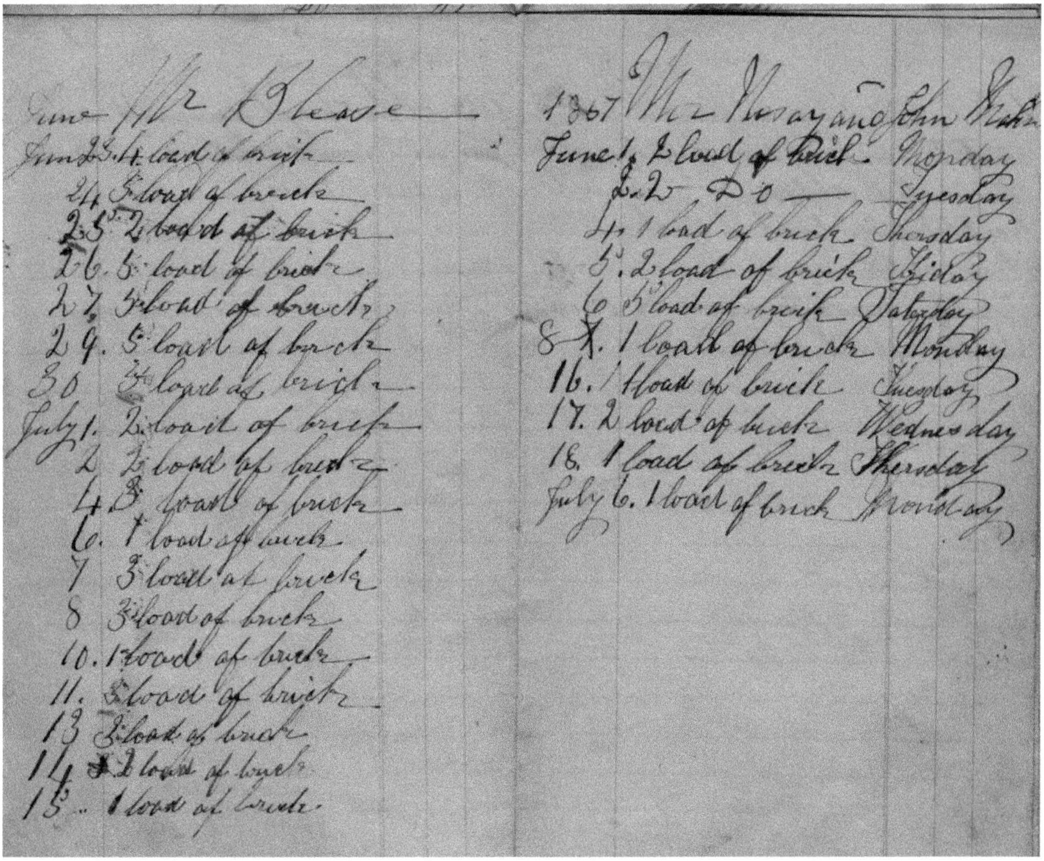
June Mr Blease
June 23. 4 load of brick
24. 5 load of brick
25. 2 load of brick
26. 5 load of brick
27. 3 load of brick
29. 5 load of brick
30 4 load of brick
July 1. 2 load of brick
2 2 load of brick
4 3 load of brick
6. 1 load of brick
7 3 load of brick
8 3 load of brick
10. 1 load of brick
11. 2 load of brick
13 2 load of brick
14 2 load of brick
15 1 load of brick

1867 Mr Hosey and John [illegible]
June 1. 2 load of brick Monday
2. 2 Do Tuesday
4. 1 load of brick Thursday
5. 2 load of brick Friday
6 5 load of brick Saturday
8. 1 load of brick Monday
16. 1 load of brick Tuesday
17. 2 load of brick Wednesday
18. 1 load of brick Thursday
July 6. 1 load of brick Monday

Extract from Book No. 1, 1857/1867.

On 23 June through to 15 July he was working for Mr Blease, carrying fifty-three loads of bricks. Again, there is no note of charges.

In between, on 6 July, he fitted in an odd load of bricks for Mr Mersey and himself.

From 16–25 July 1857, he was carting bricks for Mr Blease over a total of twenty-three loads. This was excluding 19 (a Sunday) and 20 July, so he worked eight days.

On 25 July he carried two loads of slate from Jones Yard to Smithdown Lane for 7*s*. He repeated this on 26 July for the same customer and hauled one load of white sand.

He took odd loads of bricks to Liverpool in May, June and July for Mr Hosey, with charges varying from 1–8*s* – apparently charged per load and not per day. The total charges were £1 9*s*.

Payments Recorded

In May he received £20 from John Brassington. In June, Mr Humphrey paid him £27. Both of these payments were probably for earlier work.

In July he also worked carting hay for Mr Leonid at 7*s* for a full day and 3*s* 6*d* for a part day. At the end of the month the customer paid a total of £1 5*s*. This was almost certainly during the harvest period. This connection would have been useful for obtaining fodder in winter.

Other customers also settled their accounts, totalling £34 over the two months. Over the period there were potentially forty-nine working days, excluding Sundays, and he received a total of over £84. Some of this has to refer to earlier work but pro rata he appears to have been earning over £300 per annum. This is good money by any standard of the time. Wages for labourers shot up between 1850 and 1870, but they were still lucky to earn more than £50 per annum.

The latter half of the nineteenth century saw a boom in production and labour. John himself was in the thick of it as the demand for housing grew rapidly; the bricks and stone he was carrying reflected the busy life for builders and carters.

He had to meet the cost of the horse and cart from his earnings. This included fodder (particularly in the winter months), farrier and vet costs, running repairs to the cart and horse tack and, of course, national and local taxes.

John's farrier costs for the eighteen months from January 1853 to June 1854 totalled £5 5*s* 11*d*, which is less than 6*s* per month. The major cost was new shoes. Even allowing for these expenses, John was making a good living. And he was not alone; there were at least twenty other local carters working during this period.

Book 2

This workbook is far more interesting as it contains a number of references not specifically work related. There is a reference to a 'Makin' (a relative) in Hitchin, Hertfordshire, and another reference to the Isle of Man. There is also a wealth of detail on his work as a carter.

On 6 March 1862, he hauled three loads of bricks from Barkers brickfield to Roby for Mr Hume at a total charge of £1 2 – this was noted as settled on 14 March by Annie Makin,

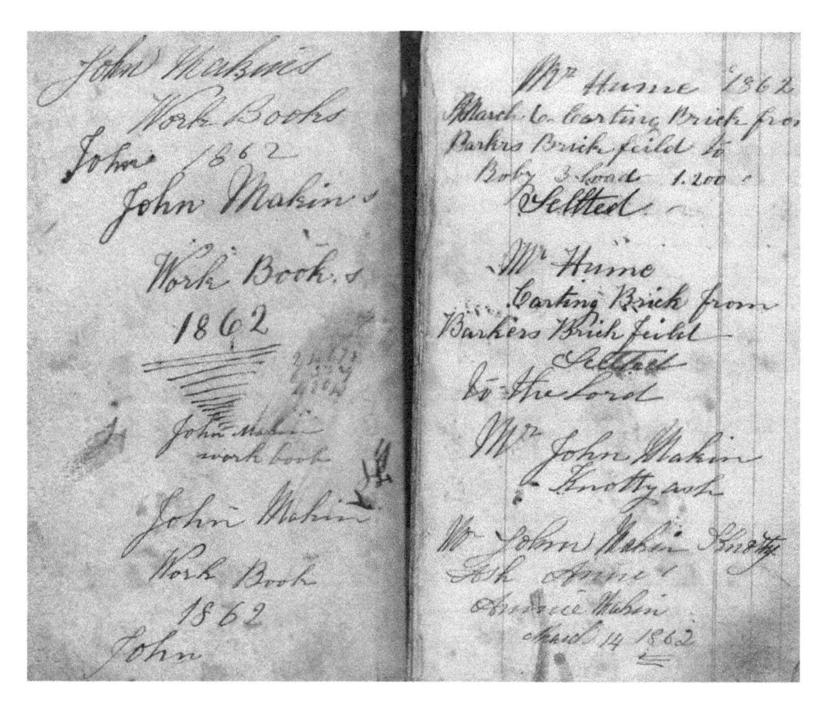
Work Book
John 1862
John Makins
Work Book
1862
John Makin
work book
John Makin
Work Book
1862
John

Mr Hume 1862
March to Carting Brick from
Barkers Brick feild to
Roby 3 loads 1.2.0
Settled
Mr Hume
Carting Brick from
Barkers Brick feild
Settled
to the lord
Mr John Makin
Knotty ash
Mr John Makin Knotty
Ash Annie
Annie Makin
1862

Extract from Book No. 2, 1862.

his daughter. Identical work for Mr Hume followed, which was charged by the load. The image shown notes the reference to his daughter, Anne, recording the settlement, as well as several repeats of his own name.

He writes a note of Mr George Howe with his full address of No. 17 St James Street, Lancaster, but includes no details of work undertaken.

From 17–19 March he is working for Mr Povall carting soil and sand at 8*s* per load.

There is also a letter addressed to 'Dear Margaret' apparently making arrangements to meet on 3 April and stay for several days. It was obviously not posted, leaving us pondering what these arrangements were and who was the mysterious Margaret.

From 4–22 April he works for a variety of clients but omits the details and the charges. Presumably these are all odd loads as he was carrying out other work. From this information we have to assume the meeting and stay with Margaret never took place, leaving an unsolved mystery.

He also makes a note of Mr Richard Lyon with an address in Throrsley, Lancashire. On numerous dates in April he was working for the Liverpool and Prescot Board carrying stone from Barkers brickfield to Whitehorse Lane and Knotty Ash, with apparently hefty charges too, ranging from 36*s* 2*d* to 39*s* 1*d* – all shown as settled.

Several pages are missing, accounting for a gap until late November when he is carting manure for Mr Williams onto the fields. This work carries on into 1863 and fits in well with the seasonal work of farmers.

In January 1863, he was working for the township of West Derby carting stone. Later in the year he worked for the West Derby Local Board carting sand and stone to Black Horse Lane.

Book 3

Moving onto the third book, this gives us the longest period of continuous records – from September 1864 to early 1867. John would now have been in his sixties and very well established in his trade.

There are many entries showing him hauling bricks in 1867, almost certainly reflecting the late nineteenth-century building boom taking place all over the Liverpool suburbs.

The records show a continuing heavy dependence on local authority work, in particular the West Derby Local Board whose jobs dominate his workload. In fact, for the whole of 1865 and 1866 he appeared to work almost exclusively for them. It seems he was happy to be largely dependent on one customer. He presumably felt confident as his invoices would be settled promptly and the risk of bad debts was low. He was mainly hauling cinders, scrapings and broken stone. Some of the work required him to pick up in Liverpool, and a number of road destinations are entered. This suggests much of the work was directed to road improvements, which was the responsibility of the local authority. There are also loads of lamp columns from Liverpool, presumably for street gas lighting. This was provided in West Derby by the Liverpool United Gas Company.

From the 1830s onwards local residents had a great deal of say in how their area was run. While most of the decision making was made by wealthy locals and senior church officials,

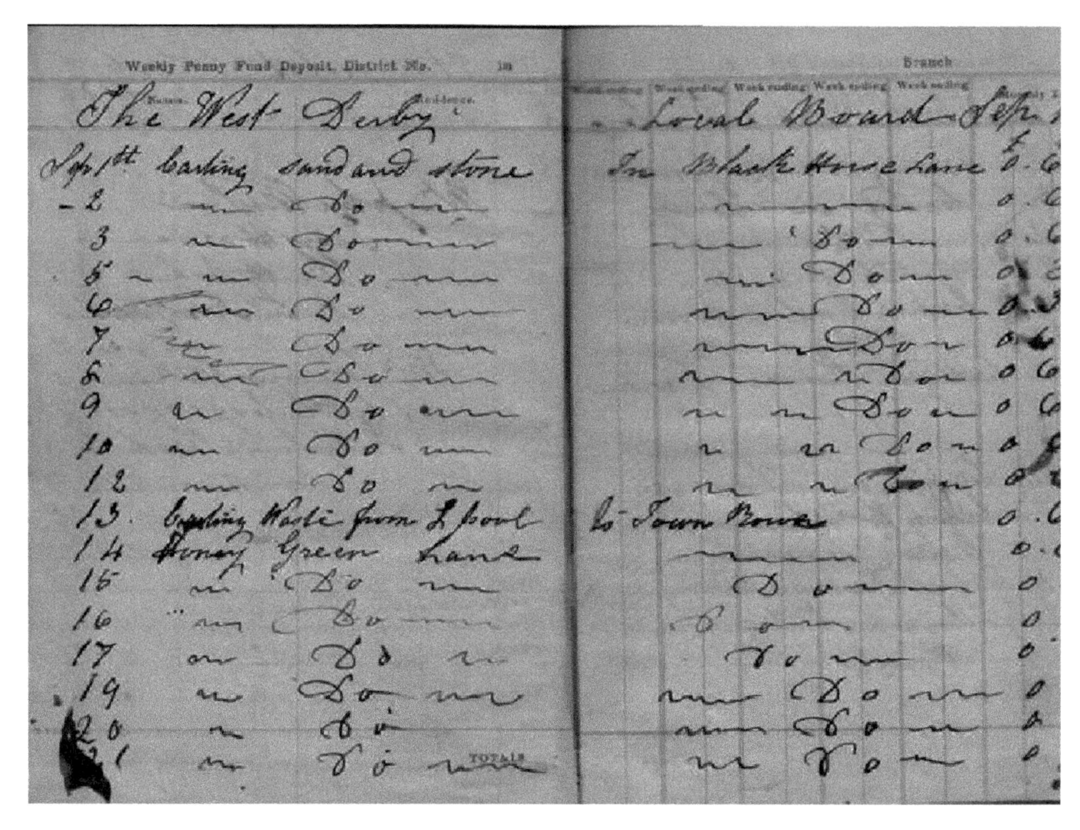

Weekly Penny Fund Deposit, District No. in Branch

The West Derby Local Board Sep

Date			Amount
Sept 1st	Carting sand and stone	In Black Horse Lane	0.6
2	Do		0.6
3	Do	Do	0.6
5	Do	Do	
6	Do	Do	
7	Do	Do	
8	Do	Do	0 6
9	Do	Do	0 6
10	Do	Do	
12	Do	Do	
13	Carting Waste from L'pool	to Town Rowe	0.6
14	Stoney Green Lane		
15	Do	Do	0
16	Do	Do	0
17	Do	Do	0
19	Do	Do	0
20	Do	Do	
21	Do	Do	

TOTALS

Extract from Book No. 3, 1864/67.

some local villagers had their say too. From 1839, West Derby had a Rural Watch run by twelve inspectors, of which six were local villagers.

The Annual Vestry was responsible for collecting government taxes and setting local taxes. In 1842, they appointed a Surveyor of Highways; however, another committee of twenty, now renamed the Highways Committee, replaced him with their own choice. The same committee appointed an assessor and collector of rates. In 1851, at a special meeting of the Annual Vestry, the composition of which was dominated by officials and nominees of the church, proposed the building of a new church. The committee was roundly criticised by locals not of the Anglican faith, who objected to being subject to charges levied by the Anglican church for its upkeep when they would never enter the building. The issue was settled as the vestry raised most of the funds themselves, and they were given both land and £500 from the Earl of Sefton to enable construction of the new church (St Mary's) to begin in 1853.

The local authority was responsible for the upkeep of highways – including street lighting, sewerage and sanitation – under the Town Improvements Act of 1847, the Public Health Acts of 1848 and 1858, and the Sewerage Act of 1865. Surprisingly, despite Liverpool's success under Dr Duncan, West Derby did not appoint a Medical Officer of Health until 1875 but appointed an Inspector of Nuisances in 1865. The local authority was very active in the second half of the nineteenth century and major improvements in drainage, sewerage and sanitation were completed.

There is no record of John Makin ever being a member of any of the local committees, but he did ensure he paid both his national and local taxes on time. For many people of modest earnings, local taxes were more contentious than national. William Pitt the Younger first introduced income tax to an unsuspecting public in 1798 at a rate of 2*d* in the pound. As we have seen over a hundred years later, 2*d* was the cost of a pint of beer in Liverpool, so at the time the rate was pretty heavy. It was always intended to be temporary in order to fund the cost of war. The 2*d* rate applied to people with an annual income of £60 and above, rising to 10*d* in the pound for income above £200 per annum. It was abolished in 1802 but was reinstated in 1803, remaining until 1816.

Income tax was to remain an emotive issue for most of the nineteenth century, although the government derived most of its income from customs and excise duties and income tax was a relatively minor element in national finances. Nonetheless, it occupied a great deal of Parliamentary time, being set at 3 per cent for incomes above £150 per annum in 1842 when some customs duties were reduced. As we note from the receipts shown here, tax was levied and paid in the 1850s/1860s but was reduced to 1 per cent in the 1870s with a promise that it would be repealed in 1874. But income tax was here to stay, and the promise was never honoured.

From the receipts shown here it is clear that income tax was not a heavy burden on the average working man. Makin has paid both year's taxes in cash. The later year (1856/7) even shows a recalculation to charge a lower amount of 10*s* 6*d* from the original £6 6*s* 4*d*. The receipt also shows the schedules on which the tax was based – A B C and D.

For the more wealthy, completing the actual tax return was a time-consuming activity in itself as the tax was designed to be levied on the ownership of assets, people (servants),

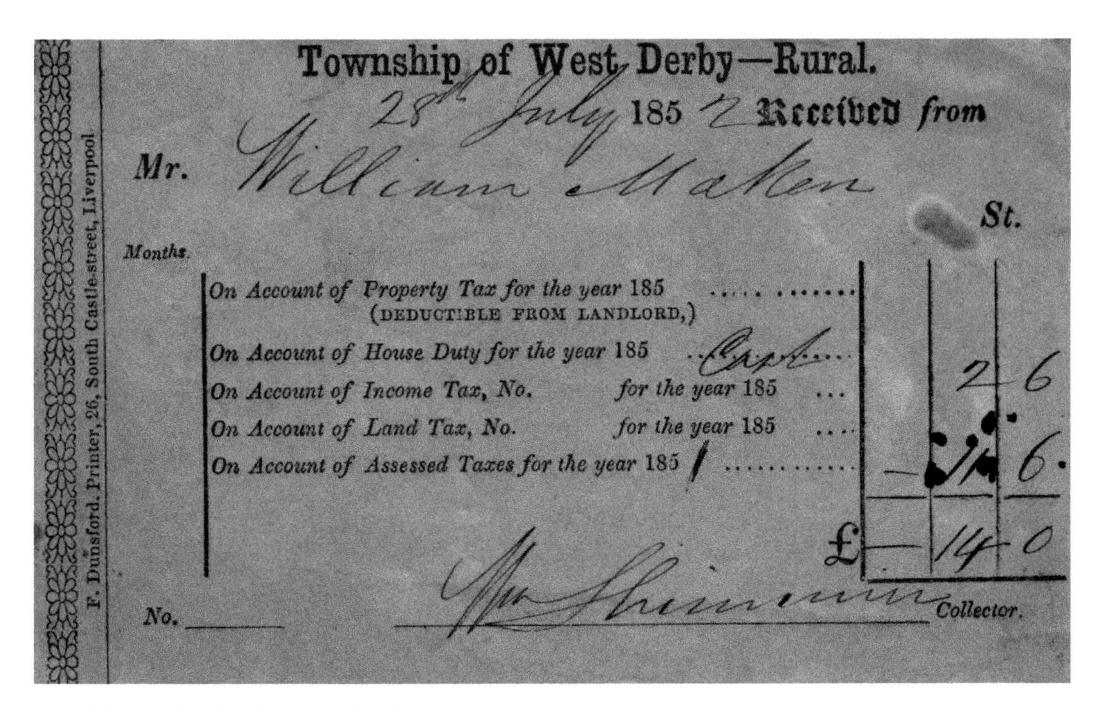

Township of West Derby—Rural.

28th July 1852 Received from

Mr. William Maken

St.

Months.

On Account of Property Tax for the year 185 .... (DEDUCTIBLE FROM LANDLORD,)

On Account of House Duty for the year 185 .. Cash ..

On Account of Income Tax, No. for the year 185 ... 2 6

On Account of Land Tax, No. for the year 185 ....

On Account of Assessed Taxes for the year 1851 .... 11 6

£ 14 0

No. Collector.

F. Dunsford, Printer, 26, South Castle-street, Liverpool.

Tax receipt for the year 1850/51.

animals (horses, mules and dogs) and goods such as carriages and traps, depending on the number of wheels and even hair powder, with the return demanding to know who actually wore it. There was also a tax on armorial bearings as well as one on second homes. The tax return comprised four A3-sized pages to be completed. The only saving grace was the tax assessor allowed the taxpayer to post his return in the tax office letterbox.

TOWNSHIP OF WEST DERBY. *(Rural.)*

GOVERNMENT TAXES FOR THE YEAR 1856—7.

To Mr. Wm. Makin Street.

	£	s.	d.
Property Tax, Schedule A, (to be deducted out of the Rent.)			
Land Tax, (do.)			
Occupation Tax, Schedule (B.)			
Income Tax, Schedule (D.)			
Income Tax, Schedule (E.)			
Assessed Taxes, including Inhabited House Duty		10	6
£			

WILLIAM SHIMMIN, Collector,
Office—1, Mount Vernon Street, Low Hill.

Payment of the Amount now due is respectfully requested within SEVEN DAYS from the delivery hereof.

(N.B.—The Present Occupiers of the Premises are liable for all Arrears of Property and Land Tax, which can be deducted from the Owner out of the Rent; and persons leaving the Township without paying the Taxes due, are liable to a Penalty of Twenty Pounds.)

Office open for the receipt of the above every Morning from 9 to 12 o'clock.

NO LIGHT GOLD TAKEN IN PAYMENT OF TAXES.

Tax receipt for the year 1856/57.

11

The Railway Age, Industrialisation and Its Impact on the Carter Industry

The railway age had a massive impact on both the UK and the world's economy, both at the time and subsequently.

Although the original impetus for rail had been to carry freight, the opening of the Liverpool to Manchester line in 1830 opened railway promoters' eyes to the value of passenger revenue. Nonetheless, freight remained a prime target, and the first goods station opened at Park Lane in Liverpool's South Docks, accessed via the Wapping Tunnel over 1.25 miles in length, providing a valuable source of freight revenue both to and from the dock system. As we saw earlier, the docks traffic was a major motivation behind the Cheshire Lines Railway's attempts to get a foothold into this traffic. Another tunnel was constructed in 1836 that was over a mile long, extending the main line into Lime Street station.

The big advantages rail had over existing modes of transport were speed and the ability to take goods directly between city centres, as well as falling freight costs due to competition.

As Liverpool was a termini of the first scheduled railway service with Manchester, it made a major impact on the North West and very soon, as railway building gained impetus, on the whole country and later the world. The 1840s were the biggest decade for railway growth and by 1850 the foundations of a national network had been laid. As we saw earlier, West Derby and the immediate area only saw direct rail links later in the century, but it did not really matter as far as the local economy was concerned, which was well served by the Liverpool and Manchester line.

For carters, the advantages of rail had little immediate direct effect, as the final miles of collection and delivery needed to be by road. However, the railway companies soon set up their own collection and delivery services, cutting out carters, entirely except in very heavy traffic periods. The bonus of this activity was employment for many more carters as the freight had to be moved locally. As the docks continued to grow and thrive, large sectors of business remained available for the Liverpool carters, who made sure they were at the forefront of opportunities.

For the packhorse business, however, the railways were the final nail in the coffin. Having already been subject to heavy competition by the turnpikes, whose improved roads enabled far more rapid transit by carts, and even more competition by the expanded canal network, the railways signalled the end of bulk movements by trains of packhorses except in the most remote areas. And so, the tinkling bells warning travellers of the approach of a packhorse train faded into history. The packhorse system of freight transport that had existed for centuries in England was now to vanish entirely.

12

Veterinarians and Farriers in the Nineteenth Century

The early roots of veterinary work can be traced back to 9000 BC in the Middle East and *c.* 3000 BC in Mesopotamia. A person named Urlagaldinna is credited as being an expert in healing animals – the earliest source to identify such a person. In more modern times the founding of the veterinary school in Lyon, France, by Claude Bourgelat in 1761 is commonly accepted as the date when the veterinary profession formally began.

Vet examining a horse.

In Britain in 1785 the Odiham Agricultural Society (Hampshire) promoted both the concept of veterinary practice and the skills of the farrier. Out of their deliberations in 1791 the London Veterinary College was founded, which gave rise to the Royal College of Veterinary Surgeons. This was established in 1844 by royal charter and ensured that the principles of teaching veterinary medicine were regulated through attendance only at specified British universities. Today the statuary duties of veterinarians are enshrined in the 1966 Veterinary Surgeon Act.

The vet's prime focus was initially the care and welfare of horses, firstly on behalf of the army and secondly for the agricultural industry and the thousands of carters working in the nineteenth century.

John Makin employed a local West Derby vet, Mr Joseph Welsby MRVCS, to take care of his horse, although the horse never appeared to have a name and is always referred to as simply 'the Black Horse'. Mr Welsby ensured the horse was treated using the knowledge of the time and was fully qualified and entitled to use the designation MRCVS. No doubt this added to the fees Mr Welsby was able to command, but John was clearly happy to have a properly qualified vet look after his horse.

Advances in medical knowledge and the ability to treat human illnesses were quickly transferred to the veterinary profession. In the 1700s and 1800s treatments for cholera, typhoid and tuberculosis were being developed. As animals suffered from many of the same ailments that humans did, it was a simple matter to transfer the technical expertise from human to animal treatment. This process has continued into the twenty-first century, enabling better diagnosis and hence treatment of animal illness and disease.

Although much of this knowledge has only been widely dispersed in the past thirty to forty years, especially advanced diagnostic equipment, the care and time vets have devoted to their animal patients has always been at the forefront of their minds.

The farrier profession was regulated well before veterinarians, receiving their royal charter in 1571. Originally the job of farrier and blacksmith were practically synonymous: both would have made and shoed horses as well as repairing tools and machinery. Today the farrier concentrates almost entirely on horseshoeing and the care of horses' hooves. For that reason, the roles of farrier and blacksmith are considered to be in separate, albeit related, trades. This was not the case in John Makin's day, with most workers claiming ability across the board, as we saw earlier.

Unlike his vet, John's farrier/blacksmith was in constant work attending to the Black Horse. The work was critical to his job, as a lame horse or a horse with worn-out shoes was incapable of working efficiently, if at all.

The original records of John's farrier costs for the first half of 1858 are reproduced here. His farrier was John Davies, and it appears he produced a half-yearly invoice from January to June. For the six-month period the total costs were £5 5*s* 11*d*. The details show regular attendance every few days, illustrating the need to ensure the horse was kept in top condition to fulfil the role. The horse would either be taken to the farrier's workshop, or the farrier would visit the horse at John's home. The record also illustrates the variety of tasks and therefore skills the farrier needed to look after a horse and the cart properly.

A number of questions arise from examining the documents. Firstly, they all relate to John's unnamed 'Black Horse' – we assume it is the same horse throughout. Secondly, if this assumption is correct, the documents cover a period of twelve years, so the horse was

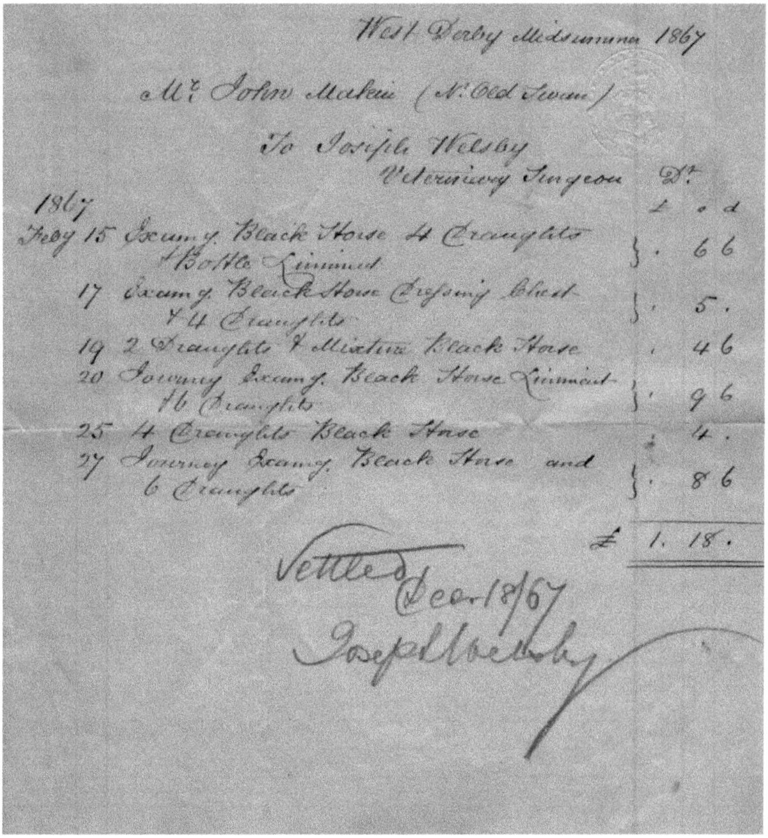

West Derby Midsummer 1867

Mr John Makin (Nr Old Swan)

To Joseph Welsby
Veterinary Surgeon Dr

1867			£	s	d
Feby	15	Examg Black Horse 4 Draughts & Bottle Liniment	.	6	6
	17	Examg Black Horse Dressing Chest & 4 Draughts	.	5	.
	19	2 Draughts & Mixture Black Horse	.	4	6
	20	Journey Examg Black Horse Liniment & 6 Draughts	.	9	6
	25	4 Draughts Black Horse	.	4	.
	27	Journey Examg Black Horse and 6 Draughts	.	8	6
		£	1.	18	.

Settled Dec 18/67
Joseph Welsby

Right and below: Vet invoices for John Makin's black horse, 1867 and 1870.

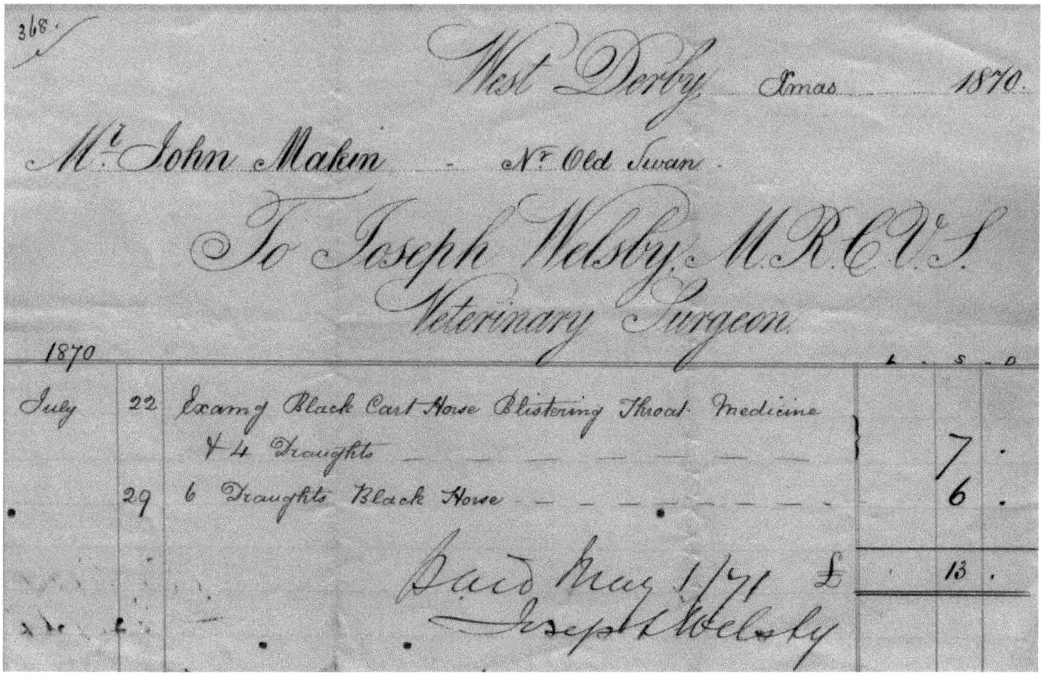

368

West Derby Xmas 1870

Mr John Makin - Nr Old Swan

To Joseph Welsby M.R.C.V.S.
Veterinary Surgeon

1870			£	s	d
July	22	Examg Black Cart Horse Blistering Throat Medicine & 4 Draughts		7	.
	29	6 Draughts Black Horse		6	.
		Paid May 1/71 £	.	13	.

Joseph Welsby

Mobile farrier at work removing a horseshoe.

at least fourteen years old, if not more as the animal would not have been used as a cart horse until it was fully grown at two years of age at least. Cart horses could work for thirty years or more if they were properly looked after and cared for, so this is not so surprising, and the evidence is that John did ensure his horse was well looked after.

The vet, Mr Welsby, also moves from handwritten invoices to more professional, printed letterheads between 1867 and 1870. Does this reflect his increasing importance in the community and rising income? There are suggestions that among his clients was Lord Derby, who lived locally and owned a number of horses both for his carriages and for sport. It is also interesting to see the credit extended by vets to their customers. Mr Welsby's bill for work he did in July 1870 was raised at Christmas in

1870 and settled in January 1871. It appears that vets regularly allowed a year's credit, with their clients settling the previous year's worth of bills each January. Obviously they trusted their customers, and the customer would probably have a large tin into which money for the vet and possibly also the farrier was deposited until payment was due.

John Makin's farrier account, 1858.

13

The Decline of the Working Horse Industry in Great Britain

As the nineteenth century drew to a close it was obvious to all, except the most die-hard members of the carter industry, that the world was changing and technical advances were accelerating.

The late nineteenth century seemed to most carters to be years of plenty, especially those working in and around the Liverpool dock system. The railways were now connected to all the docks and small steam shunters were working solidly throughout the day and into the night moving wagons. The port had continued to grow, with bigger ships and greater numbers of them arriving and departing. They needed help to bring goods to the ship's sides and take incoming cargos away into local warehouses or directly to local customers. The pressure was on from the shipowners to turn round ships as rapidly as possible, leading to queues of carters to keep a regular flow of cargo in and out.

So, there was still plenty of work for carters, and the clatter of hooves on the dock road and on the quayside was continuous. The death of Queen Victoria in 1901 and the accession of Edward VII somehow seemed to be a turning point. The Victorian age was over and a new age, the Edwardian one, was just beginning. Life for carters remained tough, but work was plentiful, wages were paid on time and there was enough in a man's pockets for a quarter of tobacco and a pint in a convivial local pub with his mates at the end of the day, so what was there to worry about? Sadly, events in Europe were soon to overtake that seemingly endless summer of 1913 in England. Within a few years countries at the other end of Europe, which the average carter had not even heard of, were about to be the catalyst for a major conflagration – the First World War (1914–18).

For the years 1870–1900, working horses remained in high demand; the total employed during those thirty years grew. However, horse numbers began to decline almost exactly from 1900. From a peak of over 1 million horses working in agriculture in 1900, a steep decline commenced. There was a minor uplift during the First World War and then it continued declining for the next seventy-five years. The prime area of decline was in agriculture. New farming methods evolved, there was an increasing use of steam farm machinery and, most of all, as the century began to draw to a close horses began to be replaced by tractors.

Throughout the century numerous steam-driven agricultural machines were developed for a wide variety of applications. The machines were quicker and therefore more productive. In some cases, farmers could hire a machine for a day and get four times the output that a horse could produce.

Back on the docks, after the First World War the motor vehicle was beginning to replace carters and their carts for the same basic reason. A driver of a lorry could do far more work in a day than a man with a horse and cart. As we saw earlier, there was a big demand for horses from the army, and the horses and carters not called up for war service were very busy on the docks. For Liverpool carters the war actually created a boom period, but it was not to last.

Men returning from the war had learnt to drive in the army and a number purchased second-hand ex-army lorries cheaply and began operating as owner drivers, especially serving the local Liverpool market. The new hauliers were competing directly with carters and began taking some of their traditional business.

No one could deny the age of the working horse, a major component of the British economy, was coming to an end. Liverpool carters were determined to continue for as long as possible and, indeed, they were commonplace for the first half of the twentieth century and right up to the 1960s. In other areas working horses remained contributing to the economy into the late 1950s. During the Second World War, under government direction, the railways took over all the horses of Garlick Burrell and Edwards, George Davies and some other smaller firms – a total of over 1,700 animals. In 1951, LMS still had eighty-five horses working in Birkenhead.

In Freshfield, near Liverpool, Dean's Farm operated a large milk round well into the 1960s. Their horse and trap (commonly called a 'float') delivered milk from their own cows either in bottles or from a large churn carried on the trap, which ladled out a gill, 2 gills or more as required. The scene of housewives attending to the float with empty jugs was reminiscent of the early 1900s, not the 1960s. However, the freshness of the milk and accompanying sales of cream and eggs were appreciated by their many customers. Coal merchants, rag and bone men, fruit and vegetable sellers, breweries and many other trades all continued to serve local customers with horses and carts.

As time passed, gradually, then with quickening pace, carters were being replaced by lorries. The carters' trade union, as we have seen, began accepting drivers into the union from 1920.

For Liverpool carters the real hammer blow was large-scale containerisation in the 1960s. Huge container ships did not require quayside work as containers were loaded and unloaded by massive cranes directly to and from lorries. As a large container ship could be turned round in one or two days, the economics were unassailable.

The larger firms such as George Davies and Jarvis Robinson among others were acquiring fleets of lorries while retaining many horses. Immediately after the war ended the haulage industry was nationalised. This helped many carters to qualify as drivers and so retain employment, but looking after an inanimate lorry was not the same as looking after a real live horse, so some left the industry altogether. Sid Welsh (pictured) remained defiant and is regarded as one of the last working carters in Liverpool. During his career Sid worked for Arthur Hughes & Son Haulage among others.

Happily, thanks to a group of dedicated ex-carters, the traditions and knowledge of the carter industry has been maintained and kept alive, ably assisted by Merseyside Museums, even if the working cart horse has been consigned to the pages of history.

Sid Welsh, one of the last Liverpool carters who was still working on the docks with shire horses in the 1960s. (Courtesy of *Liverpool Echo*)

14

The Working Horse Today

The construction of the original Mersey Tunnel in the 1930s was assisted by many horse-drawn carts, some of whom were kept underground in spite of the continuous intake of water. And yet, ironically, following the opening of the tunnel horses were banned from using it. This is a classic example of the lack of sentiment as business became much more hard-nosed. On Merseyside, after the Second World War, the change of pace accelerated and the 1950s saw a mass exodus of working horses. Many areas of employment remained, however, or were newly developed with the working horse at its centre.

Horse racing, always popular, remained a major employer of working horses. Hunters, riders and countrymen continued to regard the horse as an essential companion, whether for work or pleasure. Tourism found a new lease of life using horses on canals, in breweries and gave tourists the opportunity to ride behind a large horse. We have seen the tradition of horse-drawn trams on the Isle of Man bringing colour and old-world charm to the enjoyment of locals and tourists alike.

In the countryside ploughing competitions are held where the skills of a ploughman handling a brace of heavy horses can be admired by the public. Exhibitions of heavy horses can be seen regularly at county and town shows. There are also many examples of working horses being used for their traditional skills, including at Cambridge University where they plough the university's farm fields.

Police forces continue to use heavy horses, especially at sporting events, and the military show off their horsemanship skills at ceremonial events. Even the seaside donkeys, loved by children of all ages, continue to delight young and old alike.

It is also important that all the breeds are maintained for future generations. Reference has previously been made of the Percheron becoming endangered, as is the Przewalski, the last truly wild species of horse. Happily, there are organisations devoted to ensuring all species of horse continue to survive.

Maintaining the traditional use of the heavy horse has enabled the retention of traditional employment such as farriers, vets, grooms and horse handlers, as well as horsebox drivers specialising in heavy horses, skills that otherwise could be lost forever.

So, while the golden age of the working horse may be over, the skills required remain. And long may that be so.

Appendix I

West Derby Hundred

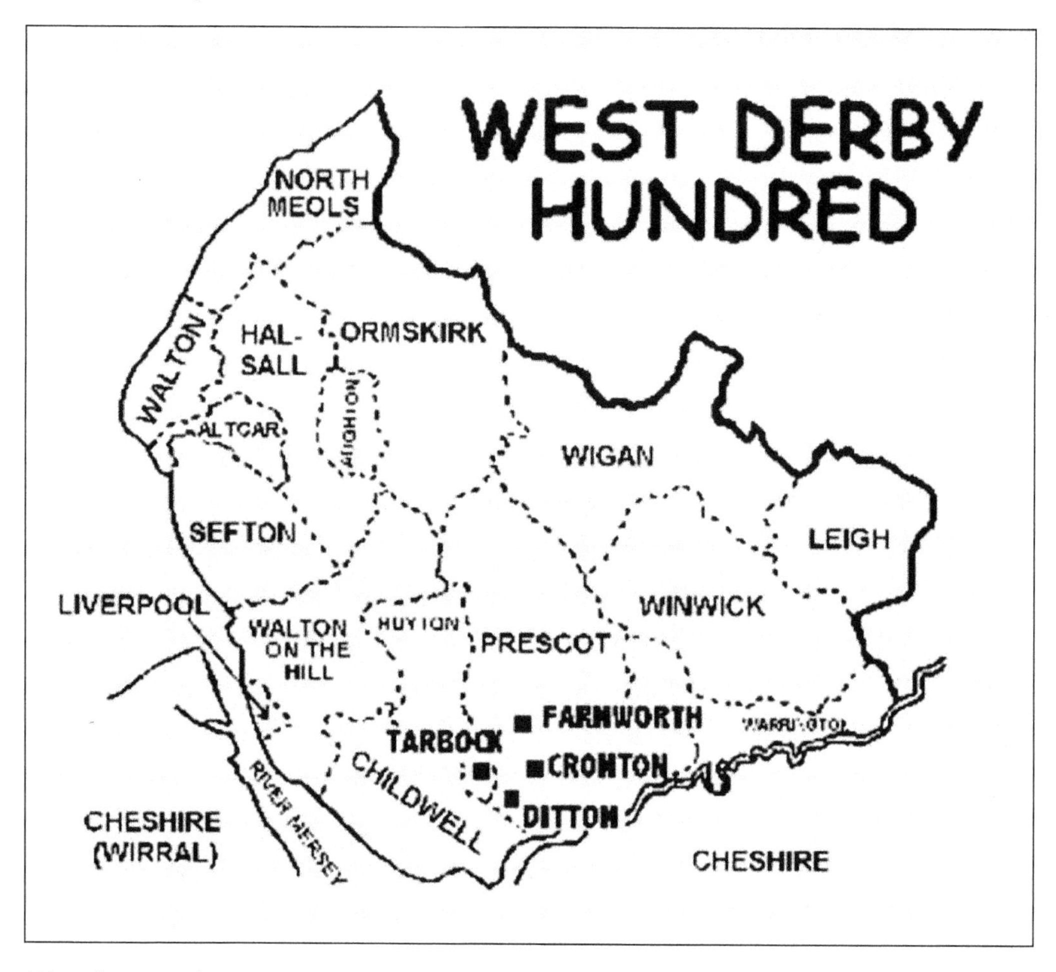

(Aboutlancs.com)

Appendix II

Ancient Map of West Derby Hundred

Appendix III

Map of West Derby, 1860

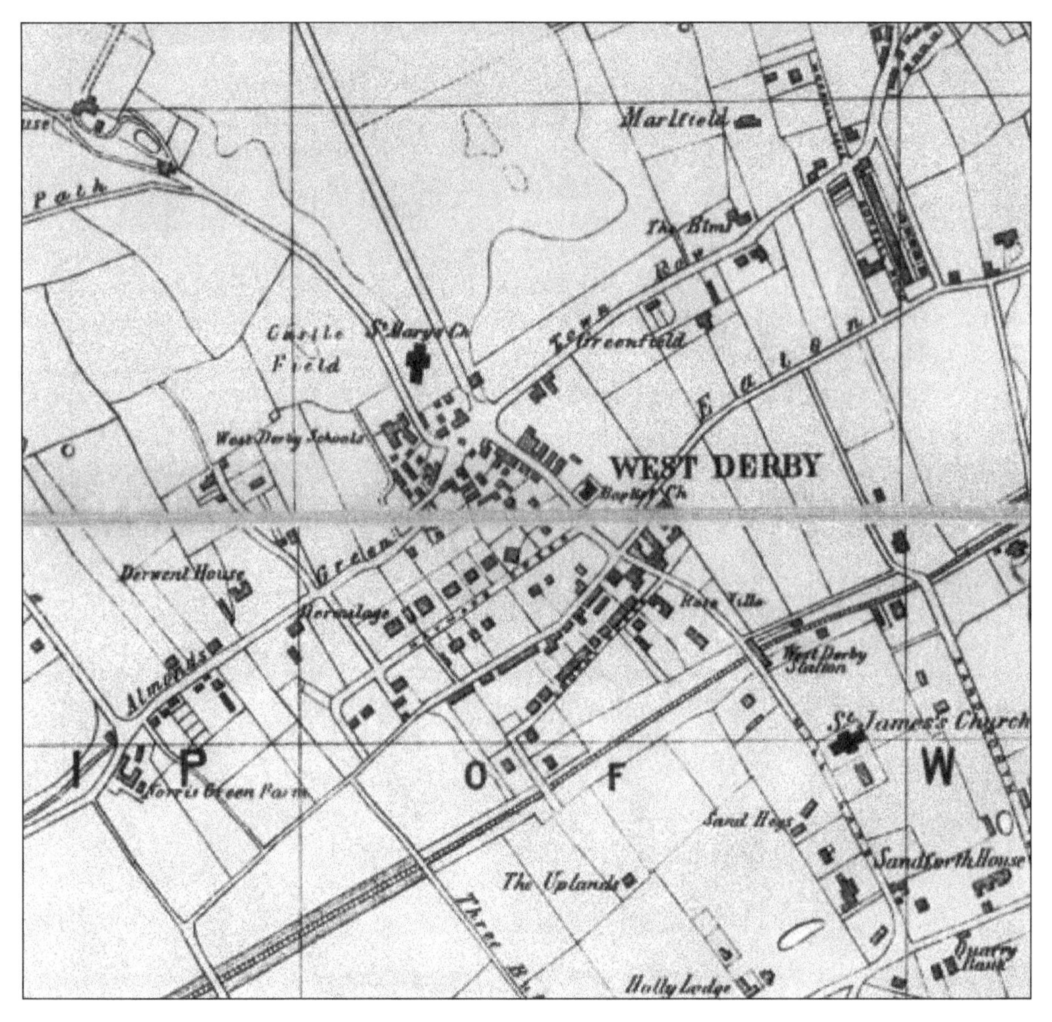

Appendix IV

Carters Rules and Regulations, 1837: By-laws for the Owners and Drivers of Carts

At a Special Meeting of a Committee of the Council of the Borough of Liverpool, held in the Town hall on Friday 24th November 1837, several By laws relating to Lorries Wagons, Timber-Carriages, Carts etc were passed, and the rates to be demanded and taken by the owners and drivers thereof, were determined upon. They contain regulations for the government of the Carter, punishing them for non compliance therewith in various penalties.

Every lorry, cart etc plying for hire to be licensed, and the owners thereof to register their names and places of abode within twenty-four hours after obtaining such license, at the Town-clerk's office, for which they will pay a fee of 2/6 for every carriage exceeding twenty hundred weight, and 1/6 for any not exceeding that weight. They are to have their names painted on each and every cart with letters of not less than one inch in height. On transfer of property, notice to be given to the Town-clerk.

The side-boards of carts to be made perfectly secure, so as to prevent rattling.

Carts not to be driven at a greater rate than a common horse walk, and shall constantly keep the left hand side of the street. No person under the age of sixteen years shall be permitted to drive a cart. All carts when loading or unloading shall be placed sideways close to the foot walk and not across the street.

No cart to stand in the street (not being in the act of loading or unloading), without some person to take care of the same.

Carters to assist in loading and unloading. Owners to deliver up the names and addresses of their drivers, upon complaint being made against them.

Every carter shall be at liberty to take into his cart the following articles and weights, and no more under a penalty for each offence, but such weights are not to be considered as applicable to any load of stone, marble, or timber to be used in the erection of any building or works, or to any load of minerals, or position, or of any machinery of manufacture, and which happens to be of greater weight than is hereafter permitted – The weights and quantities to be *one-fourth the more,* if conveyed in an four-wheeled carriage.

Bibliography

Ackroyd, Horace, *The Liverpool Stage* (Amber Valley Print Centre, 1996)
Ancestry (ancenstry.co.uk)
Auton, M., *The Development of West Derby Village 1825–1881* (hsic.org.uk)
Clark, Edward N., *The Carthorse on the Quay* (Countryside Publications, 1989)
Cooper, J. G. and A. D. Power, *A History of West Derby* (Causeway Books, 1982)
Dixon Walter, Scott, *Liverpool 1907*
Find My Past (findmypast.co.uk)
Forrest, Susana, *The Age of the Horse* (Atlantic Books, 2016)
Geographia Atlas and Guide to Liverpool (Geographia, 1923)
Herington, Pat, *Bootle in Times Past* (Countryside Publications, 1979)
Jones, Les, *Lost Wirral* (Amberley Publishing, 2019)
Radley, G., *Knotty Ash, Old Swan and West Derby* (A&R Publications, 1972)
Wooding, Harry, *Liverpool's Working Horses* (Print Origination NW Ltd, 1991)
Nixon, Ron, *Hilarious Memories of Bootle by the Sea* (1987)
Moss, W., *The Liverpool Guide 1796* (City of Liverpool Publications, 1796)
McKenzie, Neil and Herbert, *A Concise History of West Derby* (2015)
The Liverpool Mercury, various dates
Viner, David, *Wagons and Carts* (Shire Library, 2008)
Zeuner, Diana, *Heavy Horses* (Shire Library, 2004)